DRAWINGS OF A. VON MENZEL

MODERN MASTER
DRAUGHTSMEN

DRAWINGS OF A. VON MENZEL

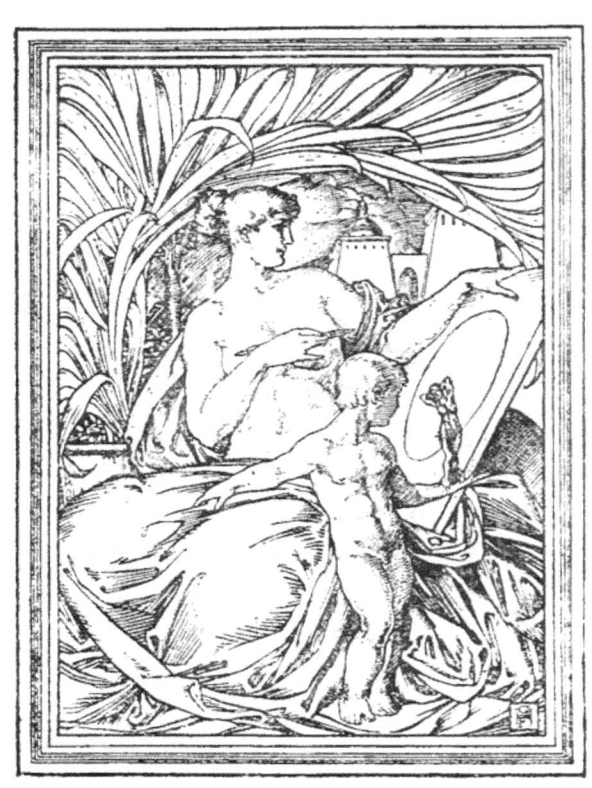

LONDON. GEORGE NEWNES LIMITED
SOUTHAMPTON STREET. STRAND. w.c
NEW YORK. CHARLES SCRIBNER'S SONS

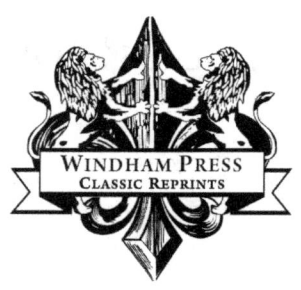

LIST OF ILLUSTRATIONS

THE DRAWINGS OF ADOLPH VON MENZEL
BY Prof. H. W. SINGER

OR two or three decades Menzel was a member of the Institut de France and an Officer of the Legion of Honour, as well as a member of the Royal Society of Painters in Water Colours and the Royal Academy of London. Yet, outside his own country, he was scarcely more than a name, except, perhaps, to the presidents and leading officers of such bodies as I have mentioned. Not long ago I found a French critic attempting to expound Menzel to his countrymen, and he had so far misapprehended his hero that he tried to make him out a sort of excellent German Meissonier. In England, too, he may be put on a line with the League of Cambrai, the Peace of Munster, the Cabal, and other such names, which you at once recognise as very important when you hear them mentioned, but about which you cannot for the life of you remember details and dates.

Almost ninety years ago, upon the 8th of December, 1815, Menzel saw the light of day in Breslau. This city was for a long time the third largest of the German Empire, without any attractions to match its size.

Menzel's father, originally principal of a girls' seminary, set up a lithographic establishment, in which the lad at an early age found an opportunity of coming into touch with the fine arts. His parents decreed that he should become a scholar, but there were many hindrances in the way of his turning student; and since he had evinced a desire to draw as soon as ever he could hold a pencil, it was easy to prepare him for the work of a practitioner in the lesser arts, if not indeed for an artist.

When Menzel was fourteen years of age his father sold his business at Breslau and migrated to Berlin. Here, too, he occupied himself with lithographic work, in which he was assisted by his son. The family had scarcely been a year and a half in the capital when the father died—in January, 1832. Menzel, only sixteen years of age, was now thrown entirely upon his own resources, and, moreover, had to help towards the support of his nearest relatives. For the sake of a living he executed vignettes for tradesmen's bills, letter-headings, designs for stencils, bottle-labels and similar hack-work, and a long period of privation and plodding began for him.

What he did at that time gave indication of what there was in the man. For where another would simply have satisfied the crude demands of the trade, he strove conscientiously to do his best and to give his customers more than their money's worth. Many of his early invitation and congratulatory cards, title pages and ephemeral designs are full of happy notions and clever allusions. Instinctively he felt that black-and-white art is a medium that lends itself to argument and discussion, and he did not miss his opportunity of communicating to an outer world what was in his own mind.

What he suffered at the time went far towards giving his character that bias which made him famous as a man. For him it was a period of what to anybody else would have seemed joyless drudgery. But it awoke no revolutionary sentiments or even feelings of dissatisfaction in him. It was then that he laid the foundation of that spirit which was best incorporated in the motto to which he remained true unto the very last day of his long life: *nulla dies sine linea*. Many decades later, when Menzel was accepted as the first artist of his country, young men occasionally applied to him for encouragement and advice—he always had a weakness for whoever considered him *the* model for the younger generation. Among these correspondents Otto Greiner—now, too, an artist of well-known standing—bewailed the loss of time that young men suffer while doing "pot-boilers" and "sweet pretty-pretty" work for the sake of keeping body and soul together, whereas, had fate been a little more kind, they might have devoted all their energies to that which is highest and best in art. Menzel's sober and impressive reply culminates in the monition: "Young man, there is no such thing as a 'pot-boiler,' there is no such thing as loss of time." He wrote: "But there is still another matter which seems to trouble you, and which is spared nobody unless he happens to have come into the world swaddled in bank-notes. This thing has many names, and a different one in every new place. I note with you it is styled 'sweet, pretty-pretty stuff'; the world in general calls it the bitter herb 'must!' or 'the dire battle of life.' . . . . There have been people, you know, who to-day count for something, and who, when they were young and helpless, had to put up with decidedly worse offers than this one you speak of. Yet everything had to be gulped down, nay, had to be cheerfully turned into an opportunity of practice, of progressing. Here

2

there is no other possible way but *to accept once for all everything as a genuine artistic problem.* You will then cease at once to consider anything unworthy of your powers; even the 'pretty-pretty stuff' will wax interesting, instructive, and even difficult. There is not much room in life for the negatory spirit of our youngsters. Your everyday surroundings should be studied best and most thoroughly. Those are the lines on which Art in former times proceeded to glory. Our old masters were narrowed down to the home circle a good deal more closely than we."

Many a man has had to suffer much during his youth, and yet had not wit enough to acquire such sage views of life's problems. But it is equally clear that Menzel would never have come by them had not fate treated him so harshly at the beginning.

Menzel's first stroke of good luck came in the shape of an offer to do up, or rather, do afresh, a set of lithographs illustrating the life of Luther. The publisher was sufficiently well satisfied with his work to accept in the following year a set of original lithographic designs by Menzel for publication. They were styled *Künstler's Erdenwallen*, which may be rendered in English, *The artist's worldly pilgrimage*, or perhaps *The artist's purgatory.* It retells, in eleven pictures, the old story of Genius, all but extinguished in infancy, trampled upon during youth, wildly idealistic, at the same time neglected and scoffed at during manhood, and finally lauded above the skies—after death. There is a good deal of bathos in such a programme, and yet it is remarkable how straightforward and simple the story is as presented by this lad of eighteen years. Those were the days when Germany was in a state of great poverty and still suffered from the effects of the Napoleonic wars. What was lacking in the way of comfort and the smiles of fortune was made up for by a slightly strained loftiness of purpose and exaltation of principle. We may presume that at that time an artist would have been downright ashamed of prosperity. This should be borne in mind when trying to estimate Menzel's album. It will then appear to be rather a simple statement, no more, and especially not the reproachful wail for which we would be inclined to regard it at the present time. The drawings received much attention, and were even distinguished by the express approbation of Schadow, then the veteran and accepted leader among Berlin artists.

There is no text; each one of the pictures has a simple title, *Germ, Trend, Compulsion, Freedom, Schooling, Trials and Tribulations, Love, Castles in the Air, Reality, The End, Posthumous Fame.* Each design, however, is supplemented by a little vignette below,

3

and this embodies the author's comment upon the situation. In *Germ* an urchin, three or four years old, is about to be beaten for having decorated the floor with the first fruits of his inventive hand. The vignette below discovers a butterfly barely escaped from the chrysalis and already beset by the dangers of the net. Hardly does genius unfold its wings before it is straightway threatened with destruction. Again, in *Reality* the artist is at work upon the portrait of an ugly old woman, while her husband lords it over him and insists upon having the picture painted the way *he* wants it, since he is going to pay for it. Through an open door we see the artist's wife with her two children—constituting the *dira necessitas* for him. The vignette below shows us an old hag trimming a swan's wings. Perhaps the bird of beautiful song would soon be ready to depart on its last glorious flight, but *Reality* intervenes and clips its wings before it can mount.

Thus, this juvenile effort displays the same spirit as the work upon which Menzel's fame in later days principally rested. Whether he illustrated his own or another's story, he embodies in various ways his own philosophical comments upon the situation depicted. Sometimes, as here, it accompanies the illustration, at others it is encased, as it were, within the illustration itself.

Menzel now attended the Academy schools, but only for a very short time. His reputation soon spread, and he received many further orders for lithographic work, while, in addition, he taught himself the technique of oil-painting.

The year 1839 represents a turning-point in Menzel's career. Mr. Weber, a publisher in Leipsic, decided in that year to issue a volume dealing with the life of Frederick the Great. He engaged Franz Kugler to write the text, and Kugler recommended Menzel as the artist most fit to design the illustrations. Menzel accepted the offer; he was still under age, and the agreement had to be signed by his guardian. In the month of March he began the study and pursuit of the one great subject which was to occupy his thoughts throughout the greater half of his career—" The Life and Times of Frederick the Second, King of Prussia."

He hunted up all the portraits of his hero that he could lay hands on, and drew from them until he knew Frederick's features and figure by heart, so that he could almost draw them in the dark. He did the same with the principal men and women at Frederick's court. He then studied the uniforms, arms, costumes and decorations of those days in the same singularly conscientious and painstaking manner. Finally, he drew all the historic localities, the rooms, houses, palaces,

4

the furniture and articles of use of the period, still to be found in them or in the museums. There are hundreds and hundreds of sketches of this kind, showing his gradual progress in acquiring a complete knowledge of every detail pertaining to the times of Frederick.

This first book, Kugler's " Frederick the Great," was completed long before Menzel's studies were at an end, of course, and it does not embody the final fruits of his researches. It contains 378 woodcuts, and we note how the woodcutters and the designer mutually trained one another to finer work as the book proceeded. Menzel gradually learned what effects could best be produced by means of woodcuts, while his assistants, on the other hand, learned, from block to block, how better to follow up the artist's ideas and intentions.

From many points of view the Kugler volume was for the artist no more than a study itself. He profited by the experiences with which it furnished him when he undertook to do the two hundred illustrations for the *édition de luxe* of Frederick II.'s own writings. This set of woodcuts is far superior to those of the Kugler volume. It represents, after all, perhaps the firmest pillar upon which Menzel's fame will rest. From the standpoint of pure draughtsmanship these designs have never been surpassed. The woodcutters who transferred them upon the block attained to the very height of excellence in facsimile woodcut. The pictures are especially interesting, inasmuch as they contain Menzel's own strictures upon the times. For they are not mere prosy illustrations of corresponding passages in the text. One of them is a portrait of the Marquise de Pompadour, accompanying Frederick's satirical imaginary epistle of this personage to the King of Hungary. Menzel renders captivatingly in line a well-known portrait of the lady and encases it in a beautifully carved frame, the different figures and ornaments of which constitute severely critical mementoes of her career and character. He includes among them a repetition of the Duc d'Orléans' famous " *petits pieds*," well known to collectors of French illustrated books of the eighteenth century. The vignette accompanying Frederick's letter to De la Motte Fouqué, in which ancient Art is compared with modern French, is not at all done in the spirit of the text. For Menzel represents a cavalier of the time comparing two pieces of sculpture, a noble ancient torso with a French affected and inflated Cleopatra; and the artist does not leave us in doubt as to his own verdict. In illustrating the correspondence between Frederick and his brother, Prince Henry, Menzel places before us the picture of Hercules and Iolas fighting the Hydra, thus apostrophising the united efforts of the two brothers to overcome their many-headed enemy, who continually manages to renew his strength. The vignette accompanying the close of the story of the first Silesian War shows a powerful hand wiping the blood off a sword with a wreath of laurels. Upon another occasion Menzel represents a wary and dangerous lion circling about an unwieldy elephant. It is the small but active kingdom of Prussia keeping the huge, sluggish Austrian Empire at bay. The final vignette (printed on the title page in the edition of 1882) shows a pair of compasses spread apart to cover just ten centimetres and squeezing a little genie. The compasses are gifted with a face which grins down relentlessly at the genie's anger at being cramped in so close a space, which forbids it unfolding its wings. In this drawing Menzel playfully alludes to the difficulty of keeping all these illustrations within the set compass of ten centimetres square.

Several other publications followed this work upon the life and times of Frederick the Great. The "Soldaten Friedrichs des Grossen" contains 31 full-page woodcuts; "Aus König Friedrichs Zeit" contains 12 marvellous large portrait-woodcuts of the King's most famous generals. The most important of all is *The Army of Frederick the Great*, including as it does no less than 436 pen-lithographs. Only thirty copies of this precious volume are in existence, and it is one of the most perfect solutions of an iconographical task that we possess. Menzel depicts the uniforms, weapons and accoutrements of almost every regiment, describing all variations in buttons, trimmings, etc., of the privates as well as of the officers. He carefully illuminated one copy himself: the other 29 were done from this by another hand.

Two things seem almost incomprehensible in connection with this publication. One is, how an artist of such powers and of such lively intellect could have had the patience to complete the task—for it took him years to do it. The other is, how he could have infused so much artistic life into it, since it was to be little more than an inventory of facts. Many of the soldiers in *The Army of Frederick the Great* are superbly drawn; the way they stand and sit, the naturalness of their demeanour, is beyond all praise. They are not modern models dressed in clothes of a bygone age. They look in face and figure and they act like the people for whom those uniforms were meant.

It was not to be expected that Menzel would rest satisfied with embodying his supreme knowledge of the life and times of his one hero in woodcuts and lithographs, be they ever so important. During the longer half of his life, black and white art was looked upon as an inferior matter, and by the time that this ceased to be the case, Menzel had virtually given up this branch of the fine arts. It was natural that

6

his ambition was to be the painter of Frederick the Great, not only the illustrator *par excellence* of his times.

His first essays in this line, *The Dinner-Party at Sanssouci with Voltaire* and *The Flute Concert at Rheinsberg*, have made him popular, though they did not in any way prepare the way for the official Court position which at the time he fondly hoped to attain. He then painted two big historical pictures, one commemorating Frederick the Great's greatest victory at Leuthen, the other his worst reverse at Hochkirch. This latter picture actually found its way into the Royal Castle, but met with so little appreciation there that it was hung in one of the offices, for the delectation of the lackeys. The fate of this picture deeply chagrined Menzel. Much about the same time he found that the large historical cartoon which he had drawn for the Kunstverein at Cassel representing the *Entrance of the Duchess Sophia with her three-year-old son into Marburg*, had been skied in a dark library. These circumstances thoroughly disheartened and disgusted him. He felt that he was wasting labours of love upon a Bœotian age. A few further historical pictures like *The Meeting of Frederick with the Emperor Joseph II. at Neisse* lacked all spirit, and the big Leuthen picture was left unfinished until his dying day. It remained in his studio, with a blank in place of the principal figure, as a lasting memento of his foiled aspirations.

When in the end other work had spread his fame, and the Prussian Court officially recognized his claim as an historical painter by commissioning him to paint the coronation of King William I. at Königsberg in 1861, his wings had been clipped—as he himself put it, in his early days—and the product was scarcely anything but a very large coloured illustration of the event, not really a painting upon a purely artistic basis.

Since Menzel's death, several people who had much intercourse with him during the last years of his life have recounted stories in which the master is represented as having disavowed his ambitions, and even as having spoken disparagingly of his historical pictures dealing with the life of Frederick the Great. It is very difficult to believe such stories as these. To begin with, it was not characteristic of Menzel to disapprove of anything that he had ever done. He was a true artist in that, for all his life work was based upon the firmest kind of faith in himself. It goes without saying that he had scarcely a word of praise for anybody's work but his own. The reader will be surprised to learn, for example, that he even decried Dürer as a poor and unsatisfactory artist. Hasty judges consider this bearing as a sign of narrow-mindedness in an artist. But it should not be looked upon in this light. Production of all kinds is a work of faith, and the

7

greater the artist the more exclusive, the more self-confident he must be. He may have many obliging phrases of easy praise at hand for the work of a confrère, but if he really at heart thought it good he would be placed in an impossible situation. For, if an artist felt that a man who is working on totally different lines from his own were right, he would practically confess that he himself was wrong. He would, in a word, have to give up working. For he could not stoop to turn copyist; neither could he, with a clear conscience, continue on paths that he had recognised as being wrong. Many weaker minds are actually placed in this predicament. A few among them give up the fight; what the remainder produce thenceforth has no serious claims upon our attention. The great artists are not subjected to such doubts and fears; they are esoteric and secluded. Each one of them furnishes repeated proof of the fact that the power of production debars one from possessing the powers of criticism.

To return to Menzel, if he actually has been guilty of such apostasy as is reported, it must have been an act of self-delusion. It may have been that he was, in a way, making a kind of virtue of necessity. At any rate, this development, if it came indeed, was late in coming. In a letter written in the year 1882, some sixteen years after these disappointments befel him, he scoffs at the idea of having lost faith in his own work. The letter was addressed to the author of a dictionary of artists, and it is a very curious epistle, written more in the style of a man of red-tape propensities than of an artist. The syntax is peculiarly involved, and the whole very wordy; it is difficult to reproduce this in the translation. It contains this interesting passage :—

"With reference to my cartoon *Entrance of the Duchess Sophia with her three-year-old son into Marburg* (drawn at Cassel, August, 1847-February, 1848), the facts are that I bought it back from the proprietors who had ordered it, namely, the Hessian Art Union. *I marvel how the fable that I had disavowed it could ever have arisen!* The truth is, I saw the cartoon again at that place eighteen years later (September, 1866), and in consequence of the absence of any suitable locality it had been hung high up on the walls of the principal Hall in the State Library, where it was covered with dust and quite in the dark. The attempt to liberate my child from these surroundings proved successful without imposing too great a strain upon my purse, and so it has hung ever since on a wall in my rooms in just the same light as the one in which I drew it."

It is curious to note what directions Menzel's genius took when once deflected from its original course. One of his biographers remarks that a casual observer must come to the conclusion that henceforth Menzel was an upholder of every new "movement" as soon as it put in an appearance. He has painted plein-air pictures, he has done impressionistic work, there are "realistic" paintings by his hand, and there is work of the kind that the recent Spanish-Italian school delighted in. It looks as if he had intended to show that he was up to any trick that came along, and as soon as ever he had proved, to his own conviction, at least, that he could equal Manet, Bastien-Lepage, Pradilla, etc., on their own ground, he totally lost all interest in their endeavours and in the style that was new for the time being.

Every one of these paintings would be a welcome addition to any public gallery, and each one is full of interest by reason of it being a Menzel. But not one of them is truly inspired, and it is not the painter in oils which posterity will cherish most in Menzel.

If, indeed, we want to get the keenest enjoyment out of his work in this vehicle, we must fall back upon such canvasses as the *Interior with the open balcony door*, which anticipates the problems that have busied later generations for years, or the *Performance in the Théâtre Gymnase at Paris*, that wonderful picture which vies in the brilliancy and fire of its coloration with the best of Delacroix. The former painting was done in 1845, the latter in 1848.

Perhaps it was upon casually coming across old pictures such as these two that the master in his last years was filled with dissatisfaction with his life-work on Frederick the Great. He would have been justified in feeling that here a great painter had been nipped in the bud in consequence of his ill-advised search for the true "historical" vein, his mistaken identification of that which is heroic in literature with that which is monumental in art.

When he painted in water- and body-colour he remained more at ease, directing his attention primarily to his media and to his style. We need make no reservation when we praise these productions. They form a kind of stepping-stone from the oil-paintings to that class of work which will interest the possessor of the present volume most. As for that, indeed, it remains to be seen whether future times will not award the palm to his drawings pure and simple when they make the final estimate of Menzel's life-work.

Their number is legion, and the array of them at the recent Menzel Memorial Exhibition in Berlin—some five thousand sheets— was simply stupendous. It is reported that he would interrupt a social gathering, or the proceedings of some important meeting, by gravely fetching out his sketch-book and pencil in order to draw a carved chair, an embroidered coat, somebody's hand, or whatever else happened to strike his eye, and the proceedings sometimes came to a standstill until he had finished. If he was not always drawing, he was at least, in every sense of the word, always ready to draw, always prepared for work. Sculptors, in order to give voice to gratitude or to set up a pattern for posterity, have erected memorials symbolising "Work." Wandering through the Menzel Exhibition one was impressed with the fact that *this* really was a monument of "Work" as powerful as any that has ever been erected, showing what sheer force of work can achieve, and that the pure will for work, when present to such a degree, is alone enough to immortalise a man.

Menzel was naturally left-handed. When already past boyhood he trained himself to use his right hand too, and from that time could draw equally well with either. It is said that he continued making the rapid nature sketches with his left, and produced the careful finished drawings with his right hand.

It was not only the mass of material that overwhelmed one at the Menzel Exhibition, the extraordinary variety of work undertaken by him was just as imposing. He had in the course of his career attempted every manner of technique. Over and above that he had attacked subjects of every description. There were quick "impressions" taken on the wing, and minute painstaking drawings, with all imaginable intermediate stages in addition. He would handle the same subject at one time with an eye to contrasts of light and shade; at another with a view to qualities of line and the presentation of a bold form; at a third with an aim at general pictorial effect. He would repeat the same study over and over again. Many people who believed that they owned *the* study for some figure in one of the famous paintings, discovered at this exhibition that theirs was only one of a set of quite similar drawings, and they could note how thoroughly Menzel went to work whenever he prepared a new picture. There were even back and side views of figures which in the ultimate painting were to be seen from the front. He did these, of course, merely in order to better understand and grasp the pose, although such supernumerary studies could not be put to practical uses. In general he strove, at least in his early days, to study his subject so conscientiously that there would be no more surprises of any kind in store for him. Perhaps the best insight into his method of work was afforded by the preparatory drawings for the Coronation picture. The National Gallery at Berlin alone possesses 170 of these. The painting includes 132 portraits, and we have Menzel's own account of the trouble he was put to in order to get all the persons shown to sit for him. If the picture failed in the end, it was not for want of self-sacrifice on the part of the painter.

It is strange to note that Menzel's eyesight and his handicraft seem to have grown stronger and more capable the older he became. Thus it transpired that, unlike all other famous artists, his handling did not grow broader and freer with age, but, on the contrary, went more into detail; he finished everything off more and more carefully to the very end of his days.

The present selection has been made from the portfolios that were found in his studio after Menzel's death. There were twenty-nine of these portfolios, containing over four thousand drawings, covering all periods of his life, and the selection is a fairly representative one—as representative, perhaps, as fifty drawings can be made to be out of a total of several thousands. Every one of them is here reproduced for the first time, except the title page for an album; I considered myself particularly lucky to be able to include this. It is an excellent specimen of that particular style of designing in which Menzel delighted and surpassed. It goes hand in hand with *The Maurergesellenbrief*, *The Shooting Diploma*, *The Pater Noster*, etc.

This drawing really requires a longer commentary than it is possible to devote to it here. Its theme is the various paths of an artist to glory, the propitious and unfavourable experiences that befall the many candidates, the opinions of the public at large and of the professional critics. Some of the aspirants try the "short cut," by currying favour with a powerful academy or a famous master; some by simply employing their well-filled purses, while others try to edge themselves in by hook or by crook. Various are their professed ideals as they journey onward to the common goal, and scathing is their opinion of the other man's ideal. In the midst of all this turmoil the child of genius sleeps secure in Nature's arm. She will take care of him when time comes. He need not worry about the ways and means.

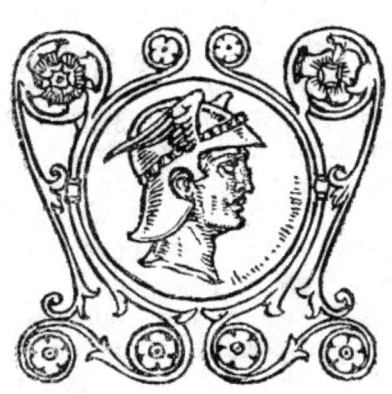

ILLUSTRATIONS

PLATE I   FRONTISPIECE

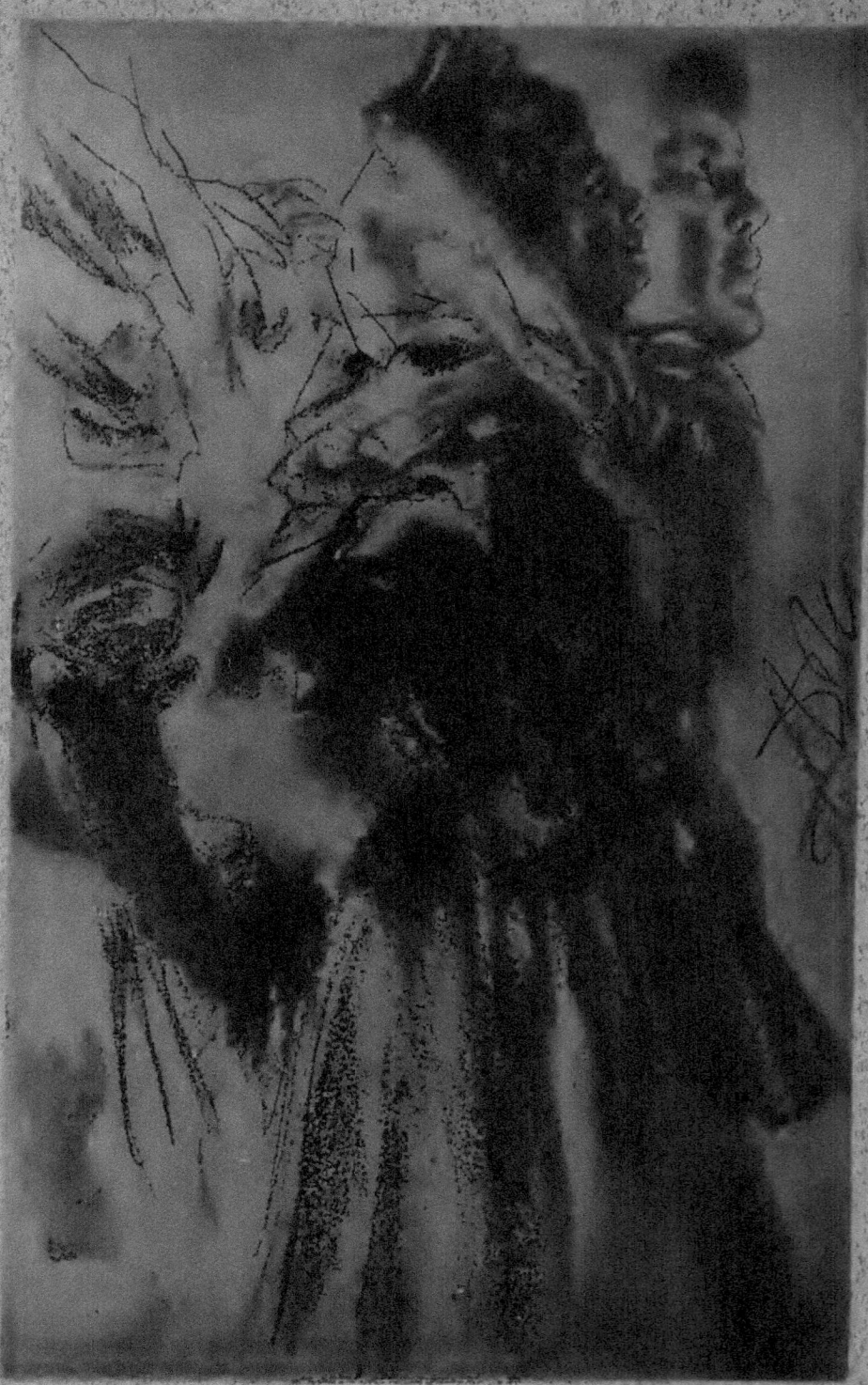

A WOMAN WITH A SHAWL AROUND HER HEAD

PLATE II

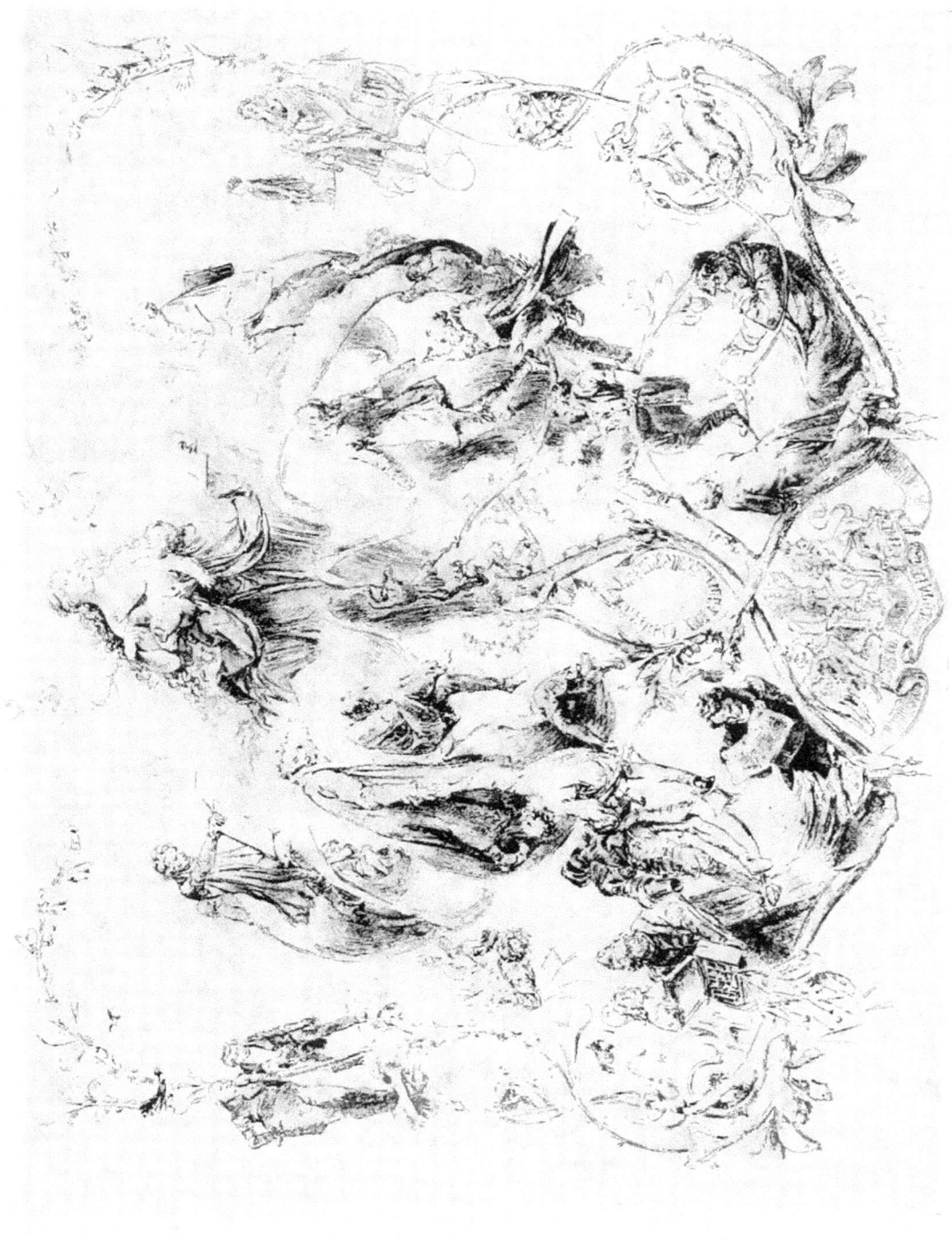

TITLE PAGE FOR AN ALBUM

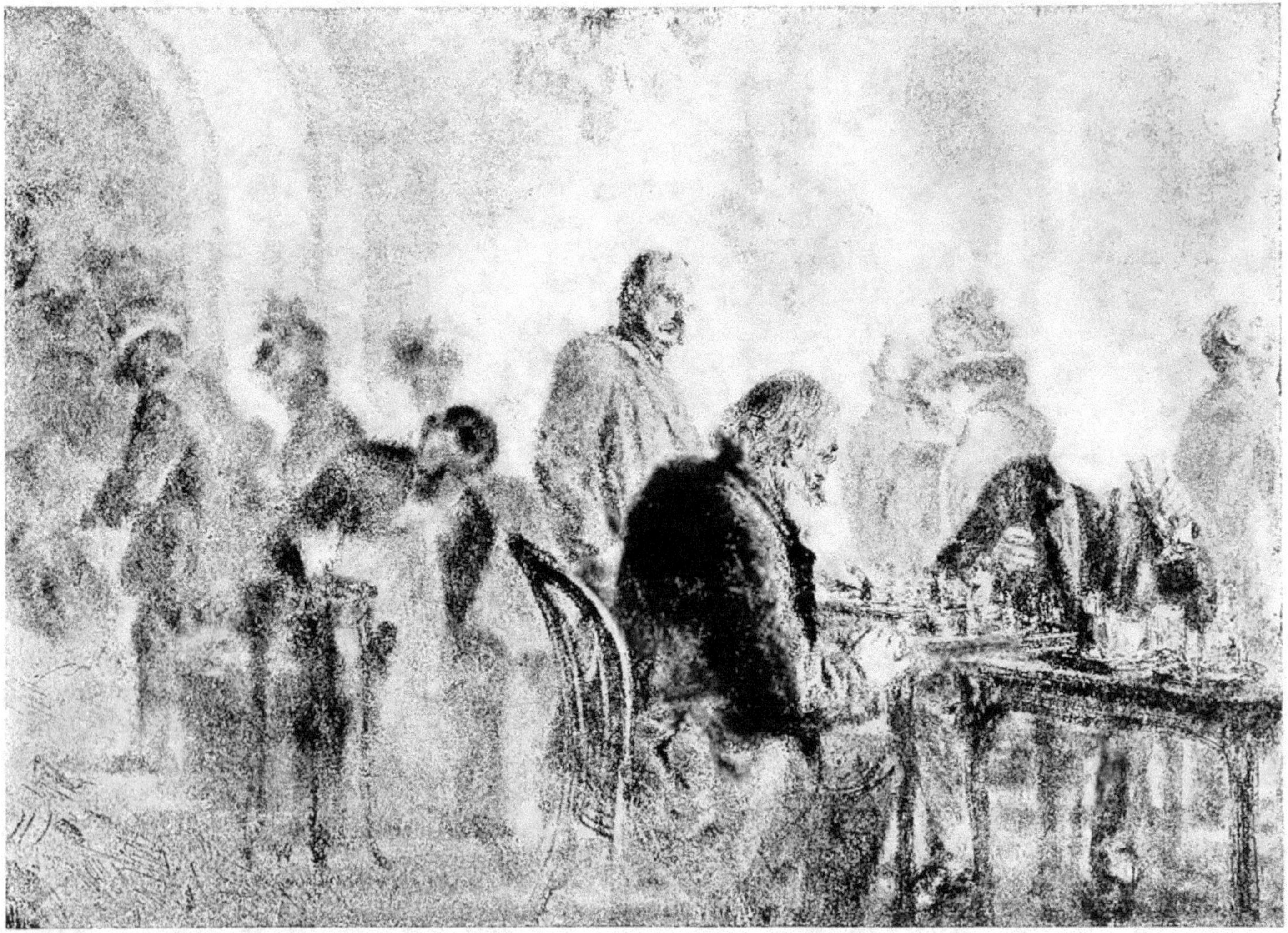

PLATE III

CAFÉ, WITH CHESS PLAYERS

PLATE IV

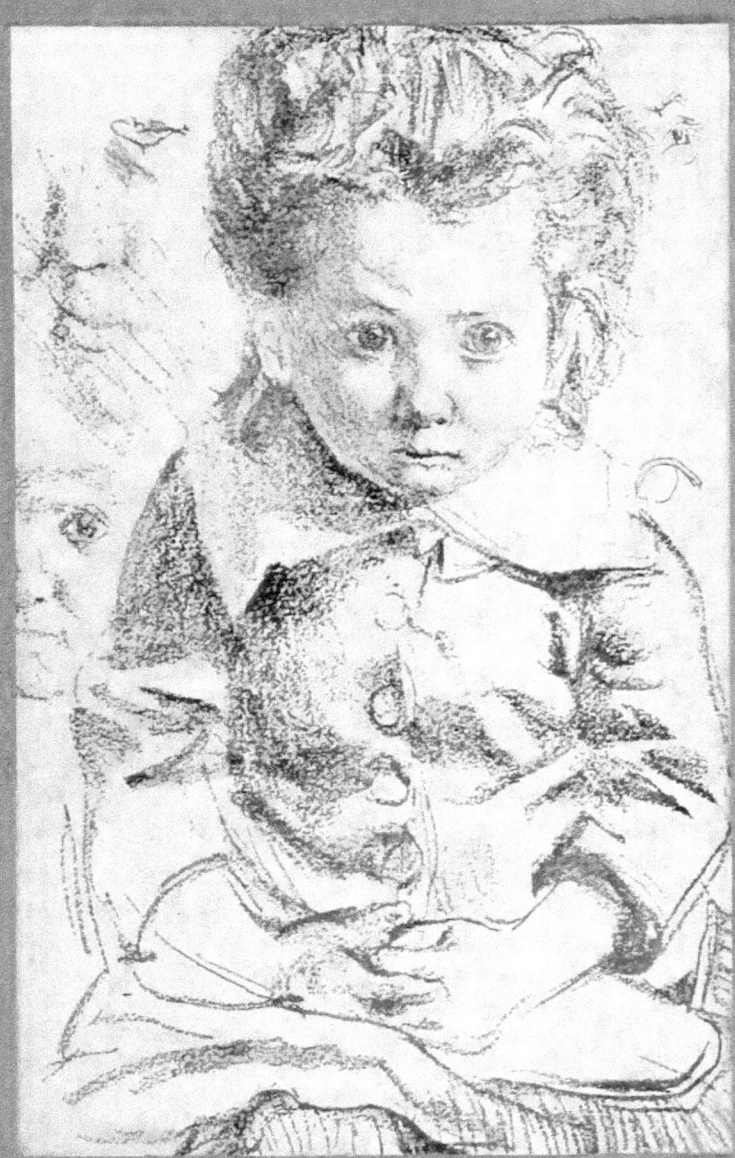

A CHILD WITH HANDS FOLDED

PLATE V

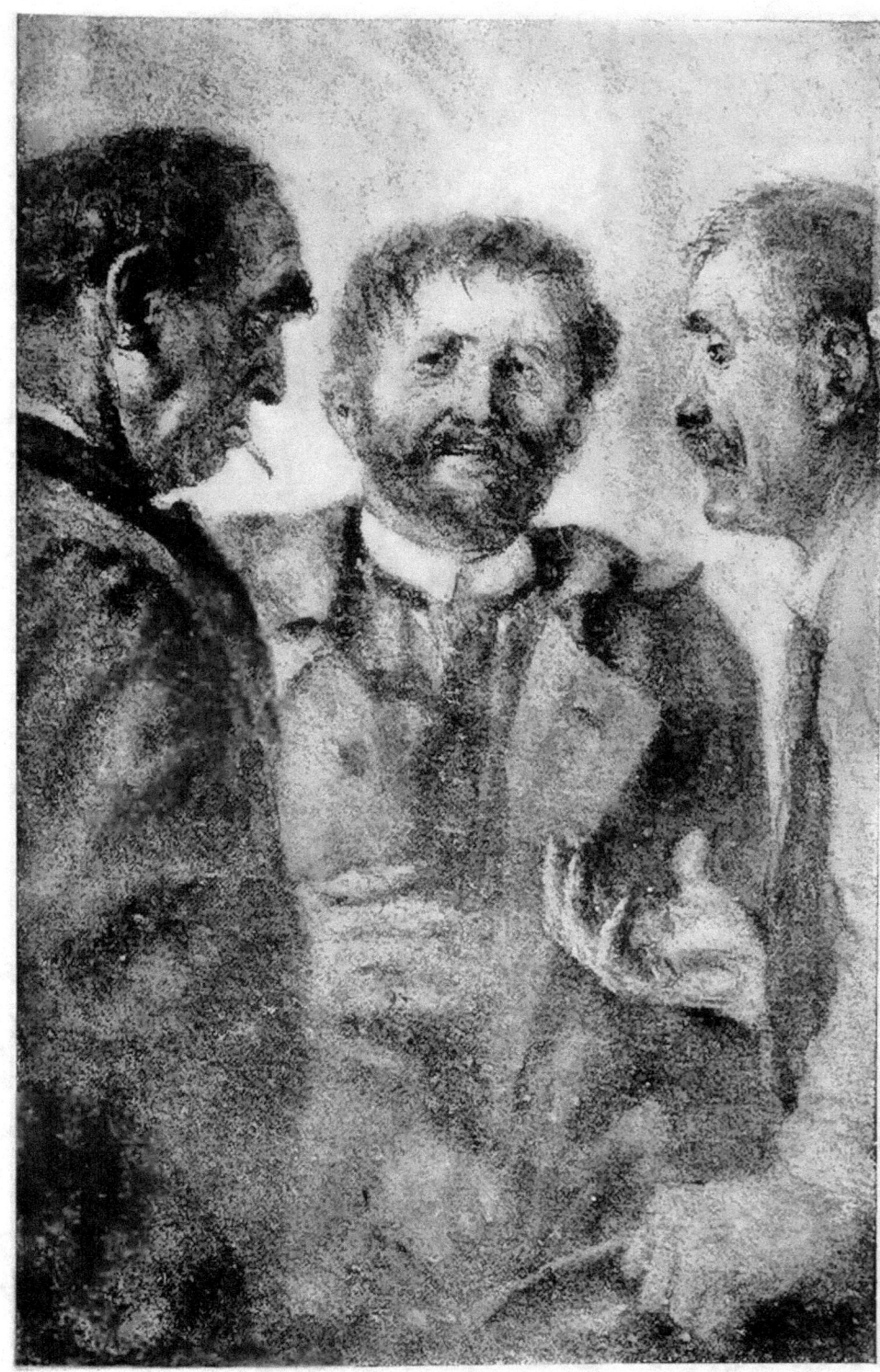

THREE MEN DISPUTING

PLATE VI

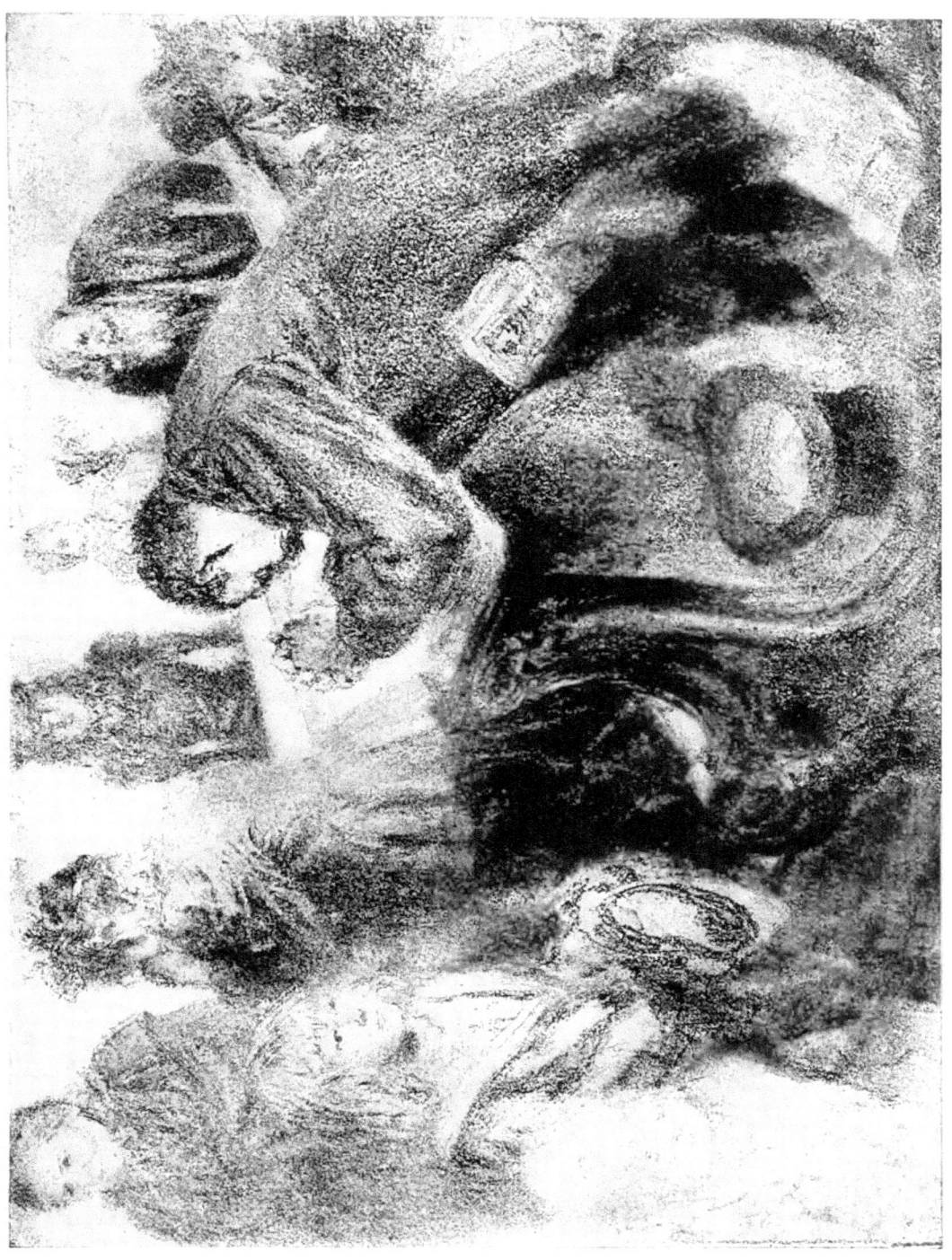

PLATE VII

CHILDREN SLEEPING

PLATE VIII

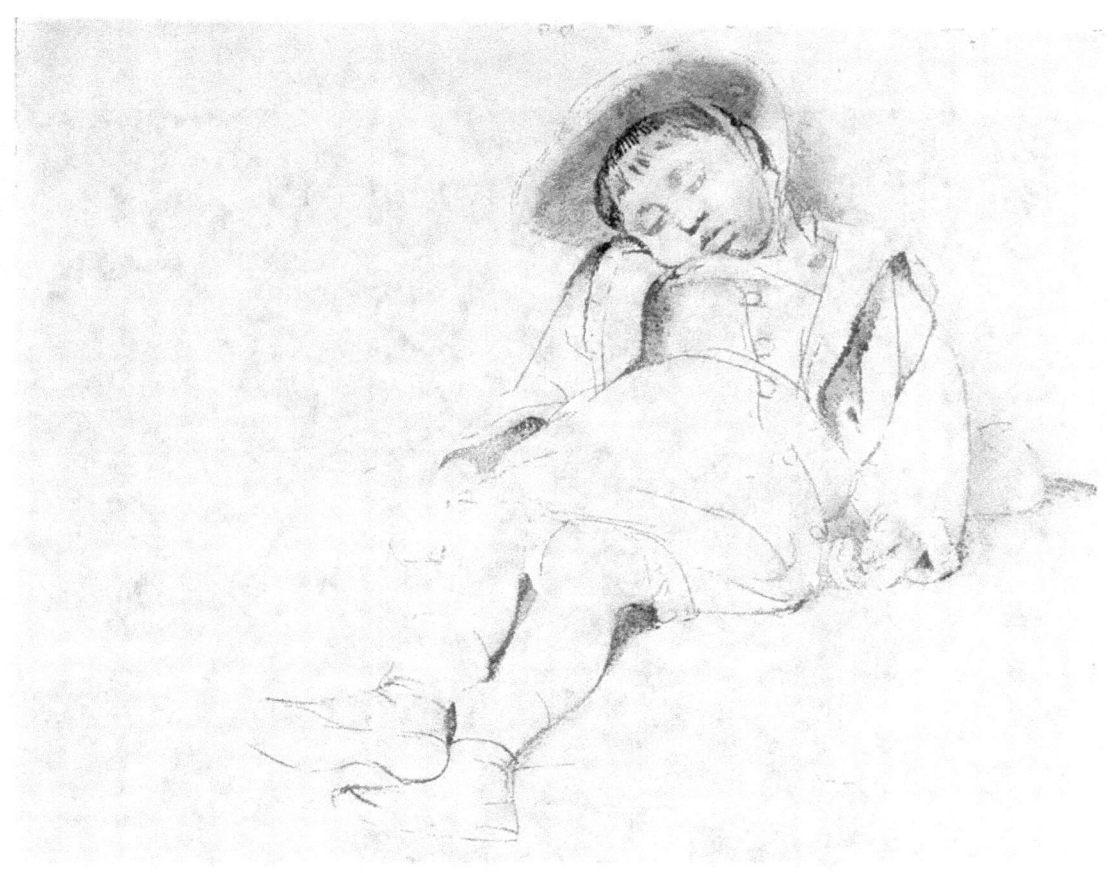

A CHILD FALLEN ASLEEP

PLATE IX

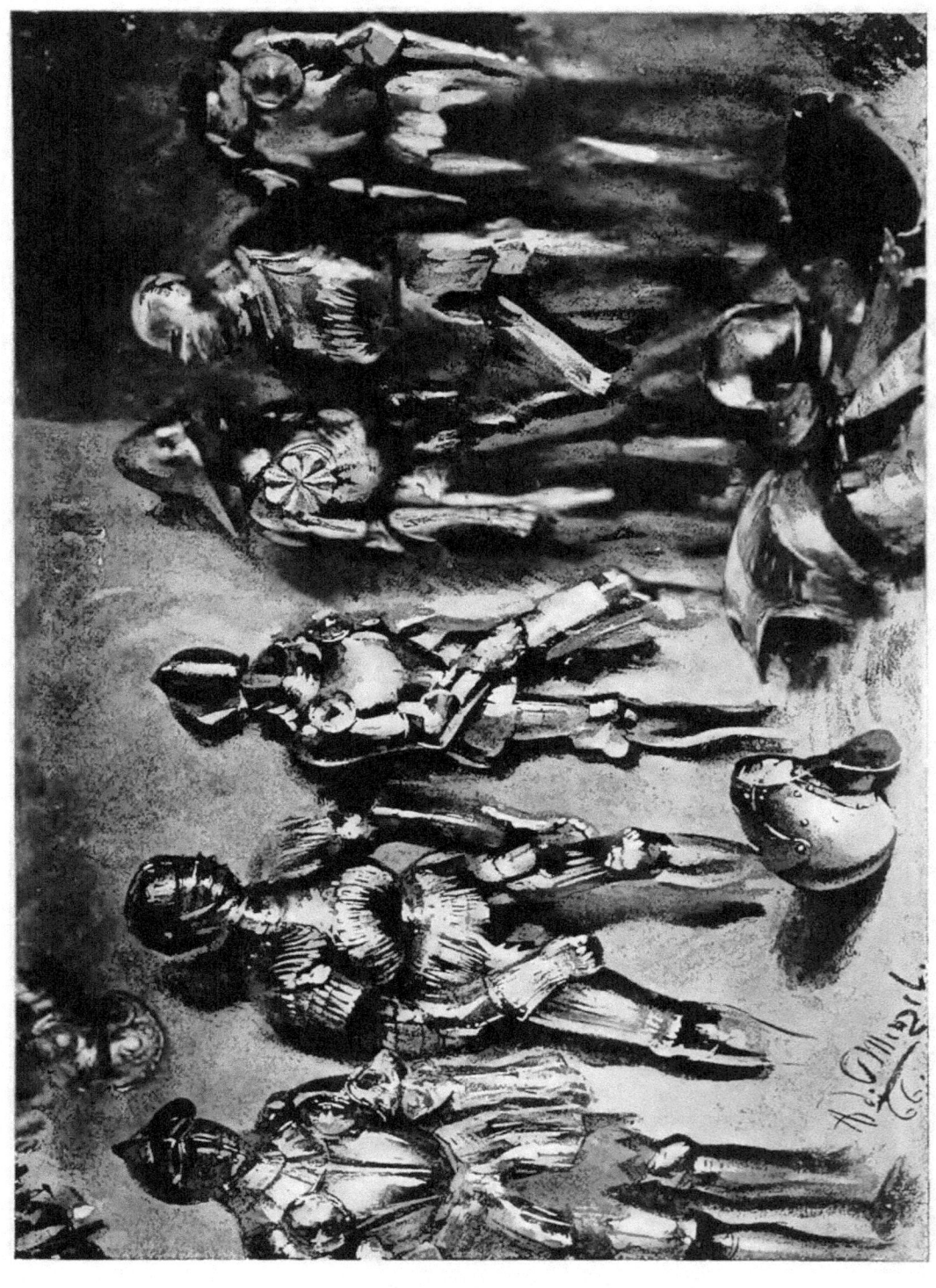

STUDIES OF ARMOUR

PLATE X

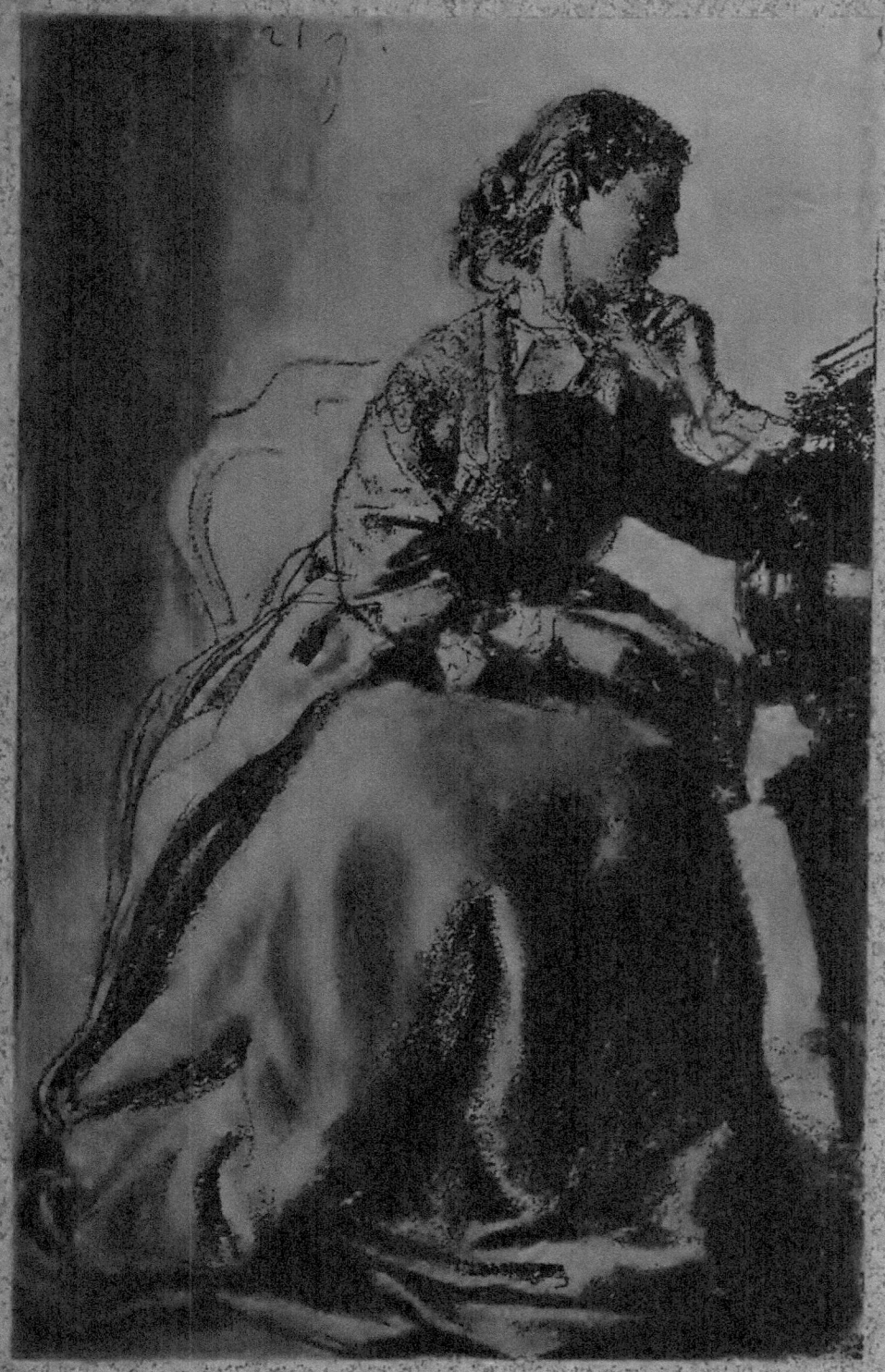

LADY SITTING BY A PIANO

PLATE XI

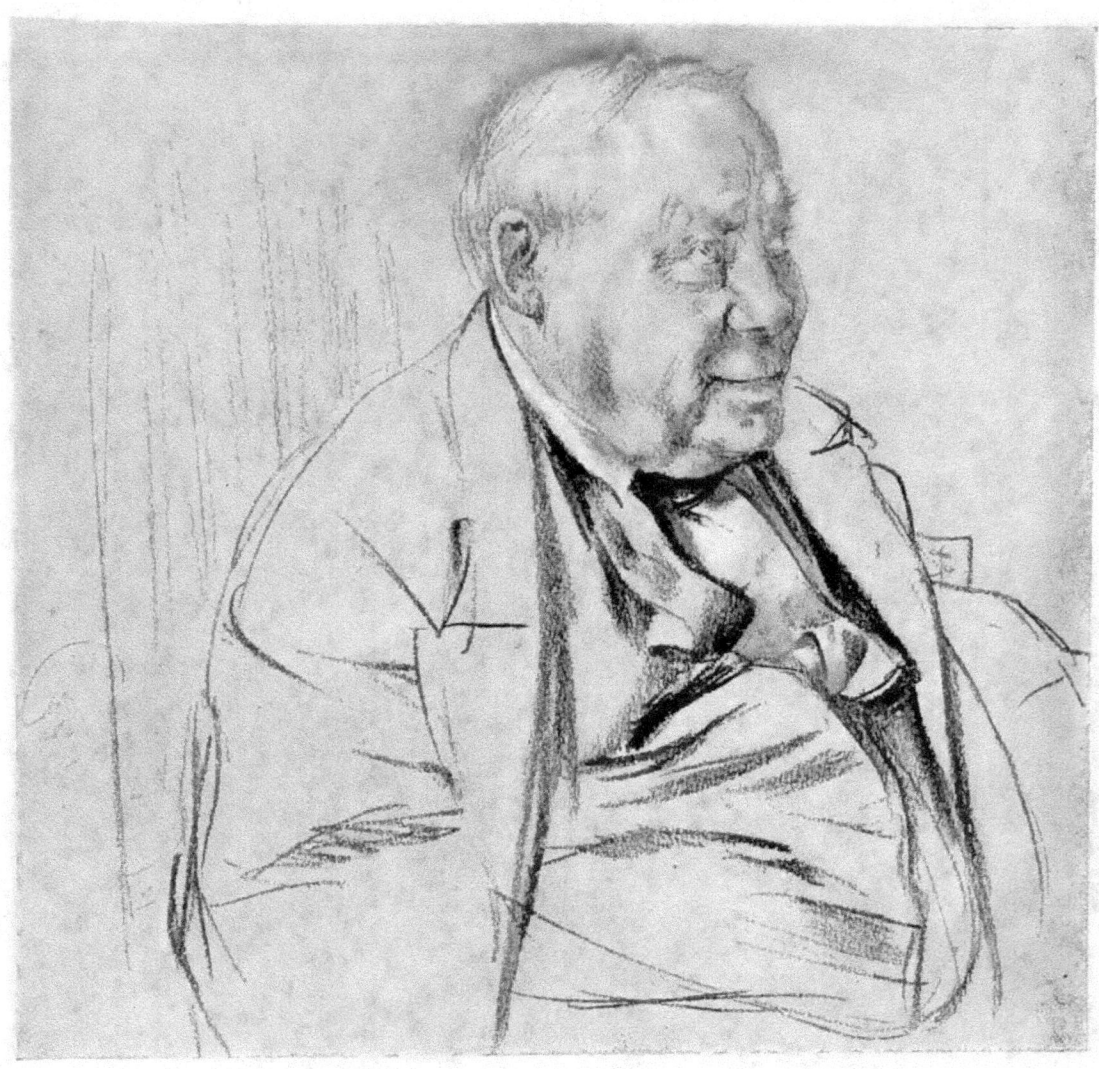

PORTRAIT OF A MAN

PLATE XII

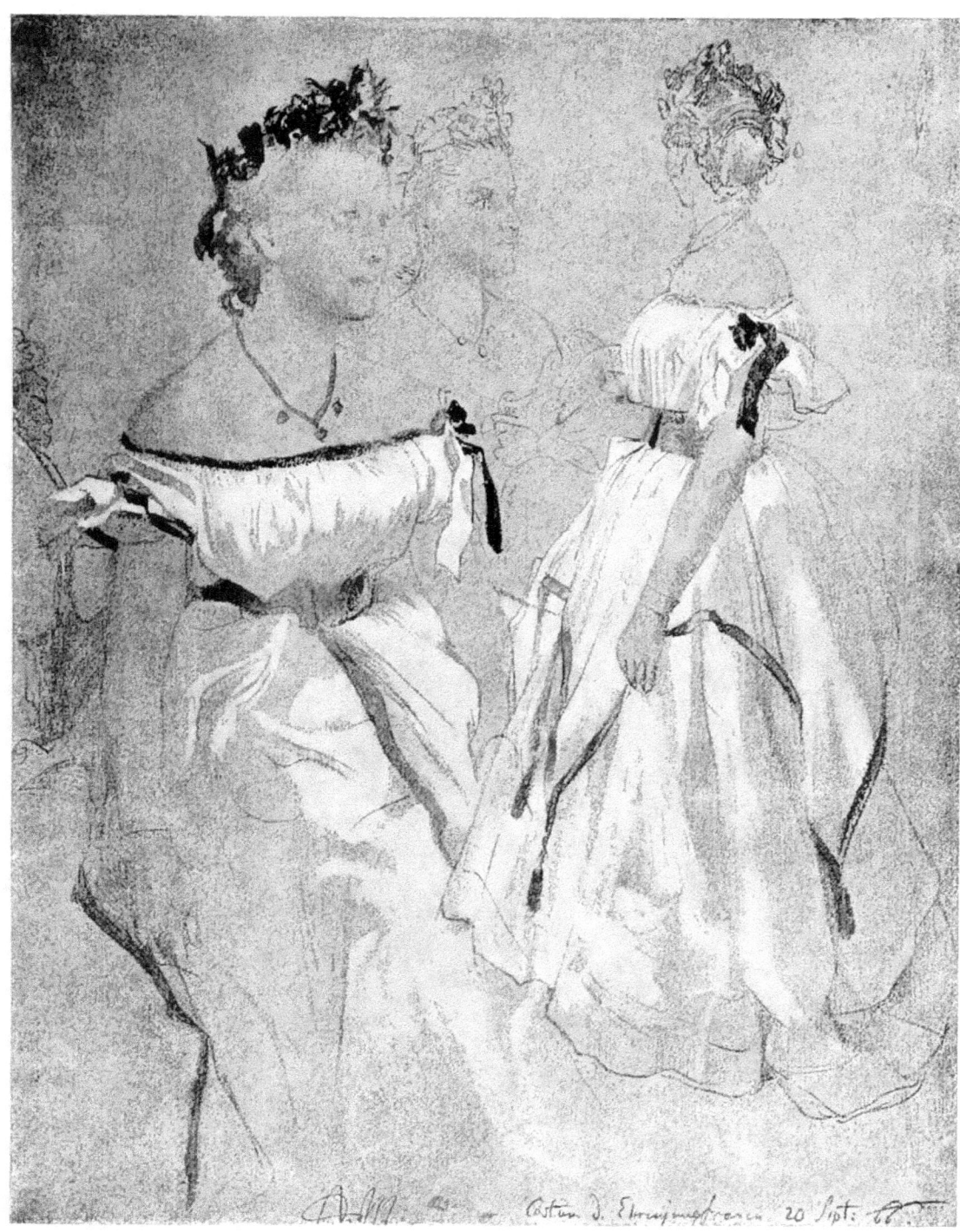

COSTUME STUDIES

PLATE XIII

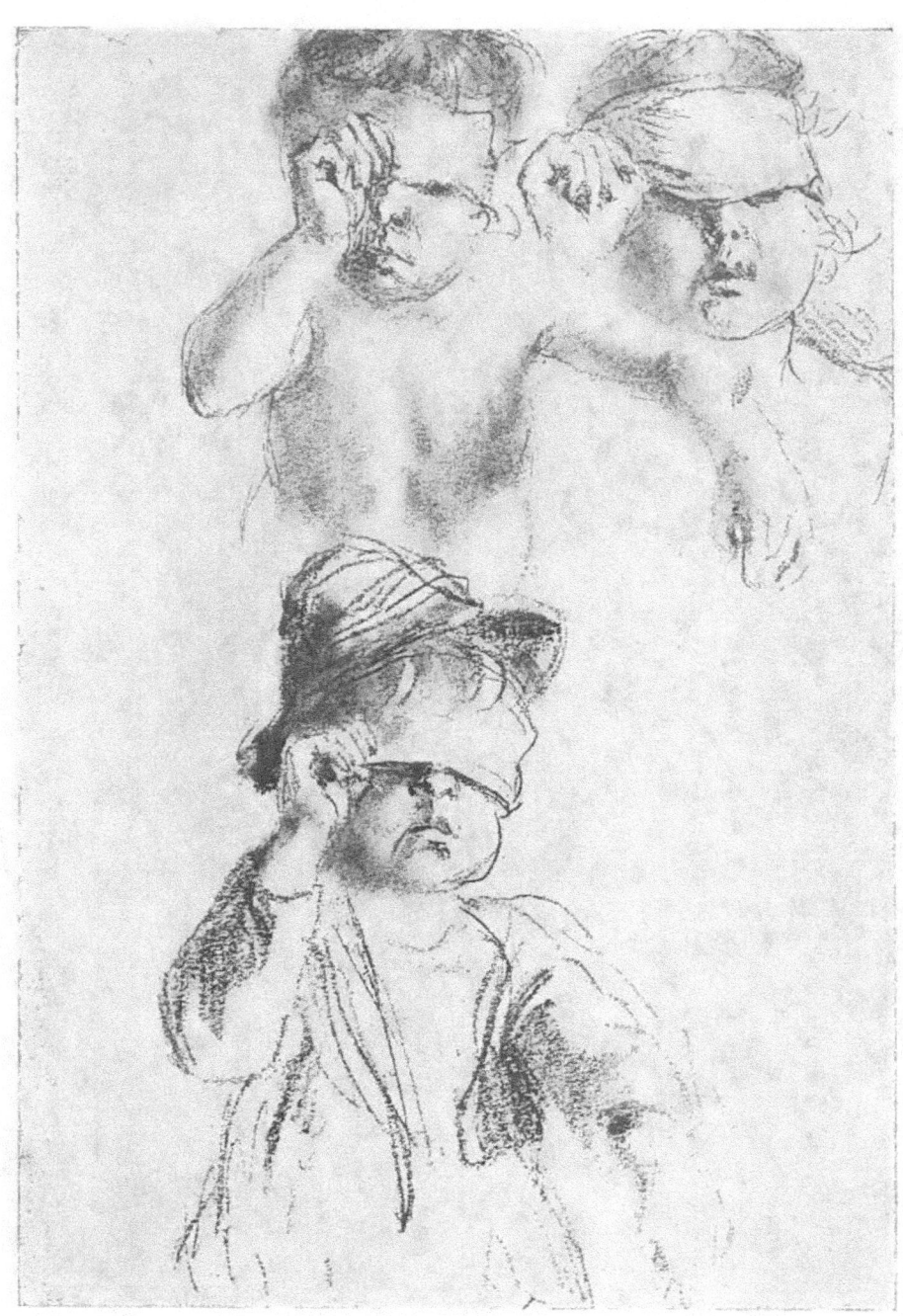

CHILDREN BLINDFOLDED

PLATE XIV

PLATE XV

PLATE XVI

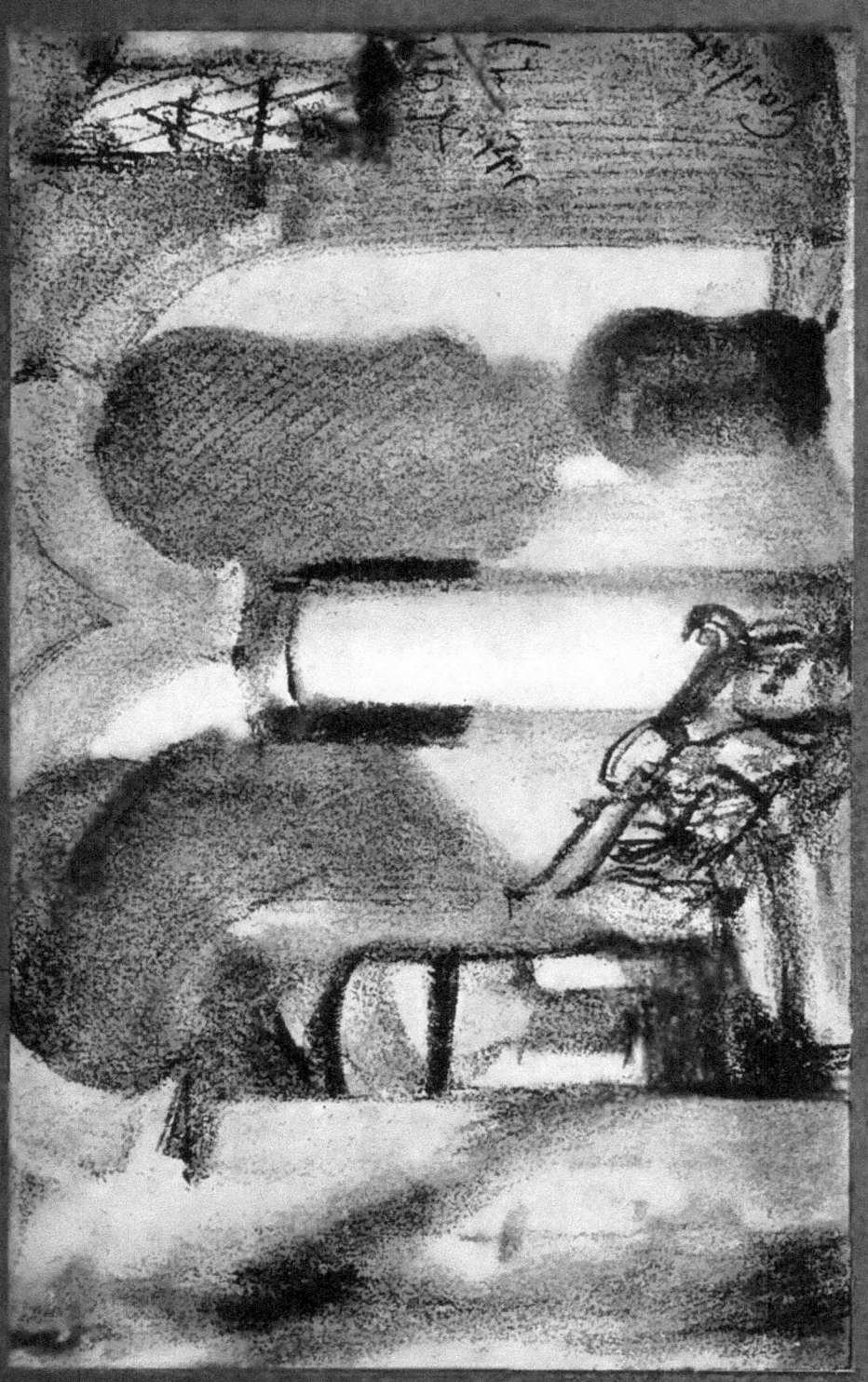

INTERIOR OF A HOUSE, AT SALZBURG

PLATE XVII

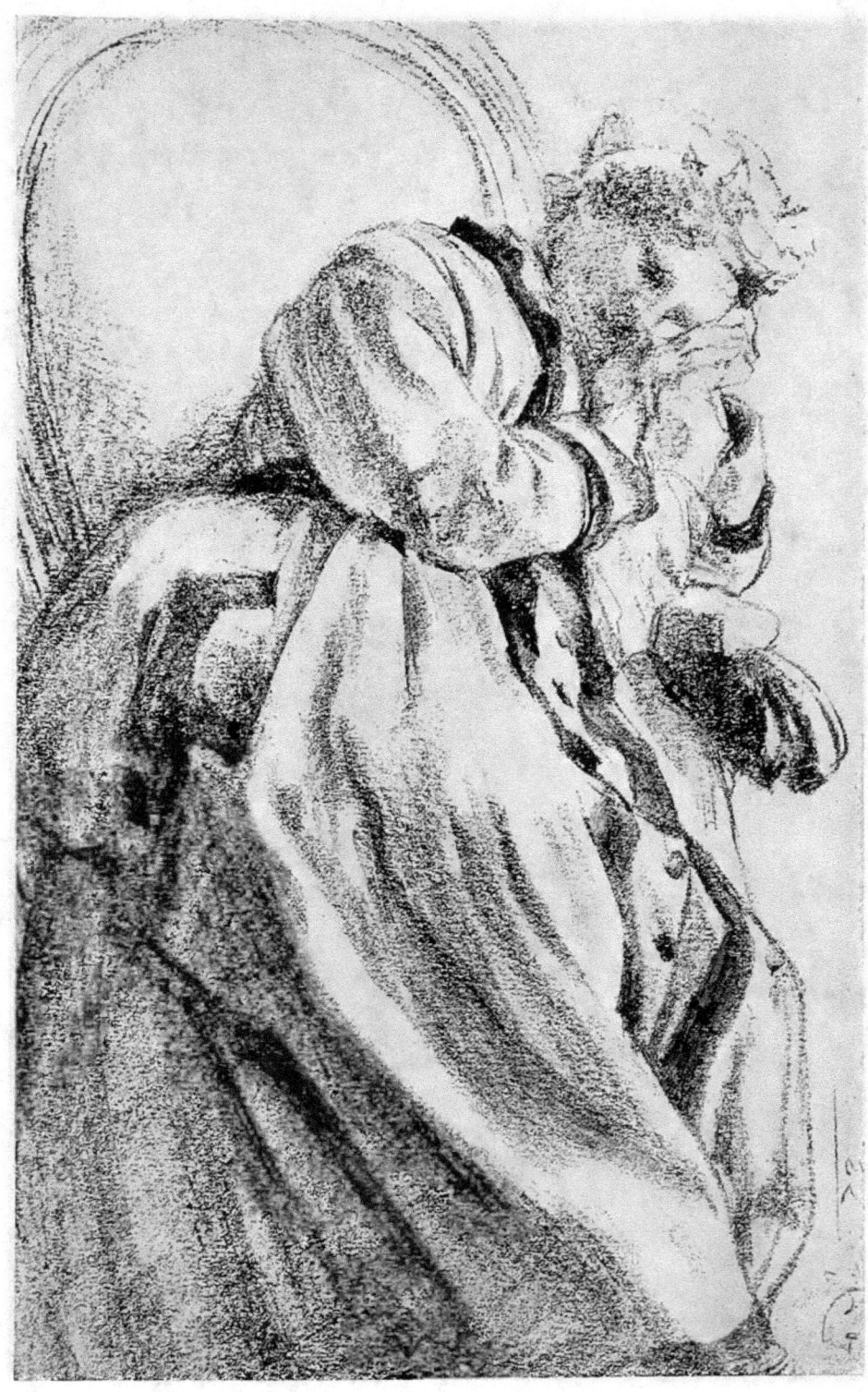

LADY IN AN ARM CHAIR

PLATE XVIII

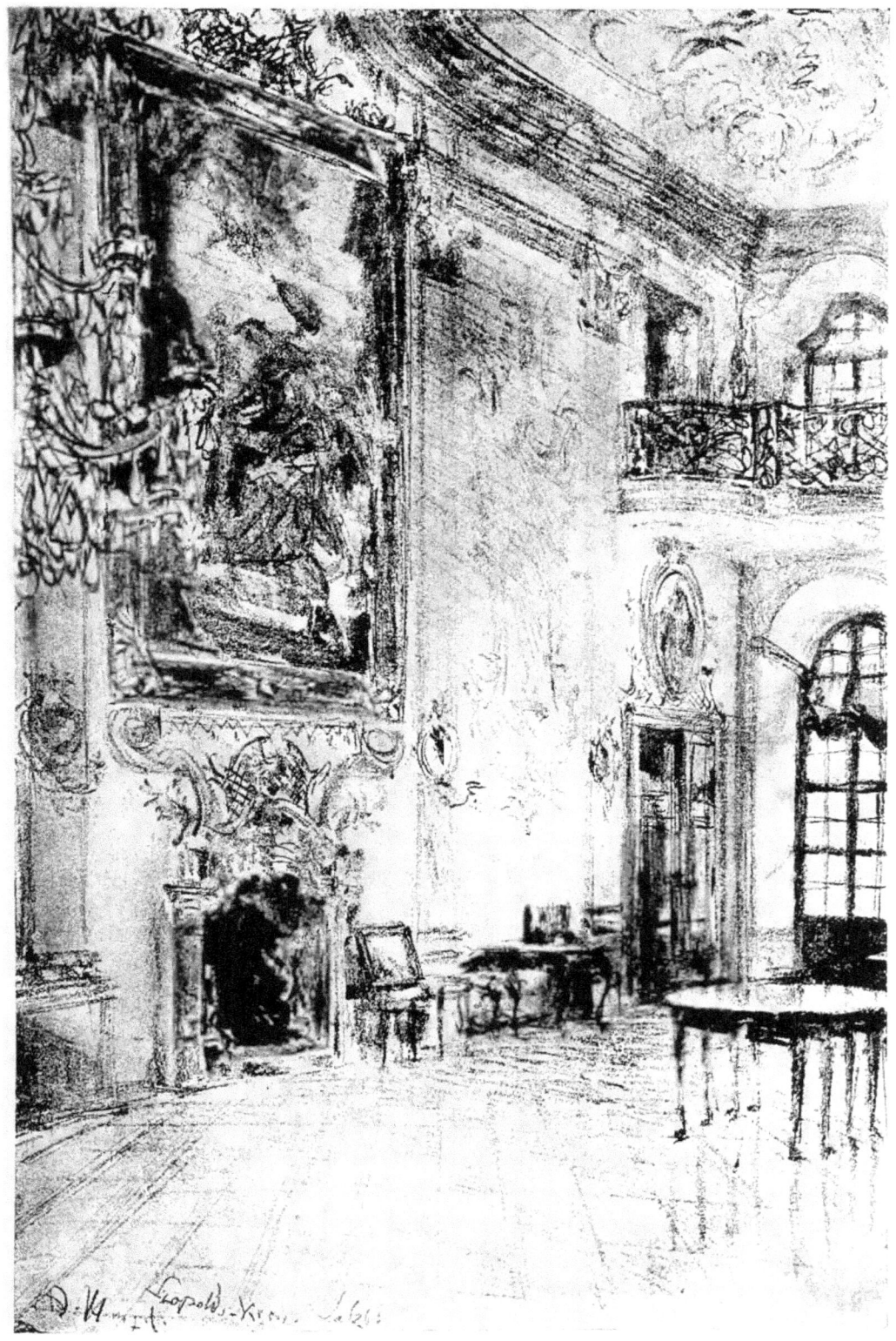

HALL IN THE LEOPOLDSKRON-PALACE AT SALZBURG

PLATE XIX

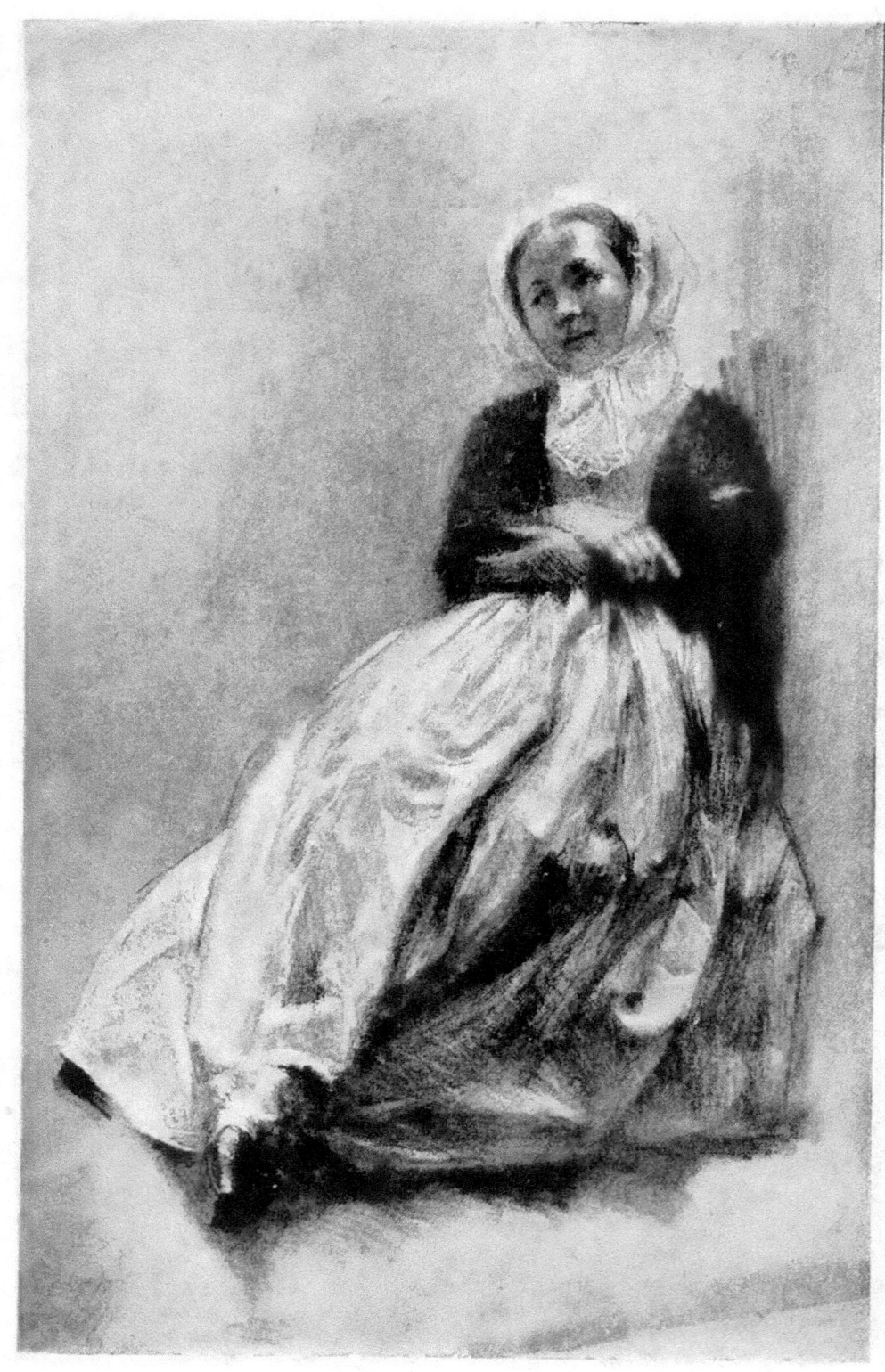

YOUNG WOMAN SEATED

PLATE XX

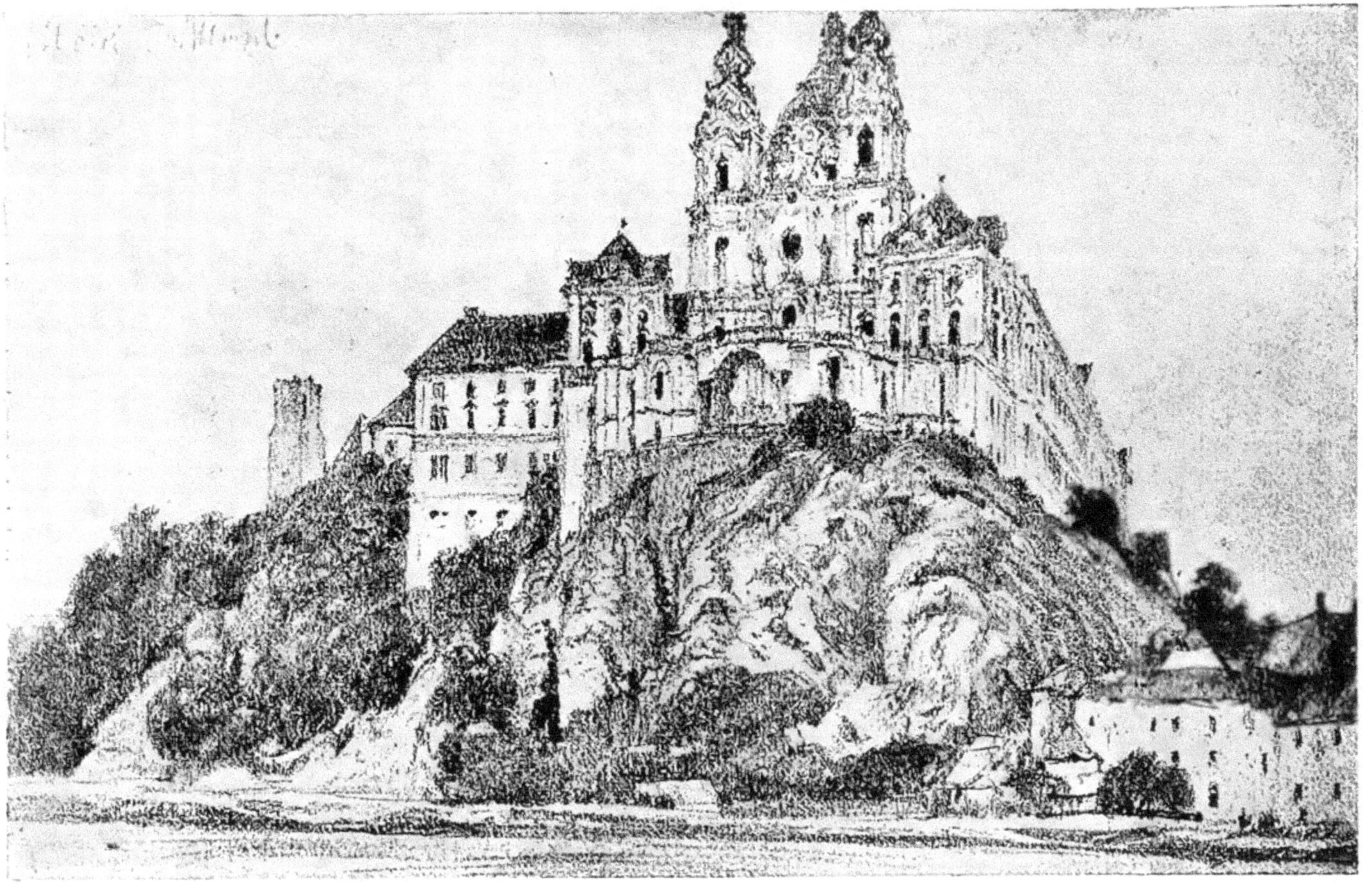

THE MONASTERY AT MELK ON THE DANUBE

PLATE XXI

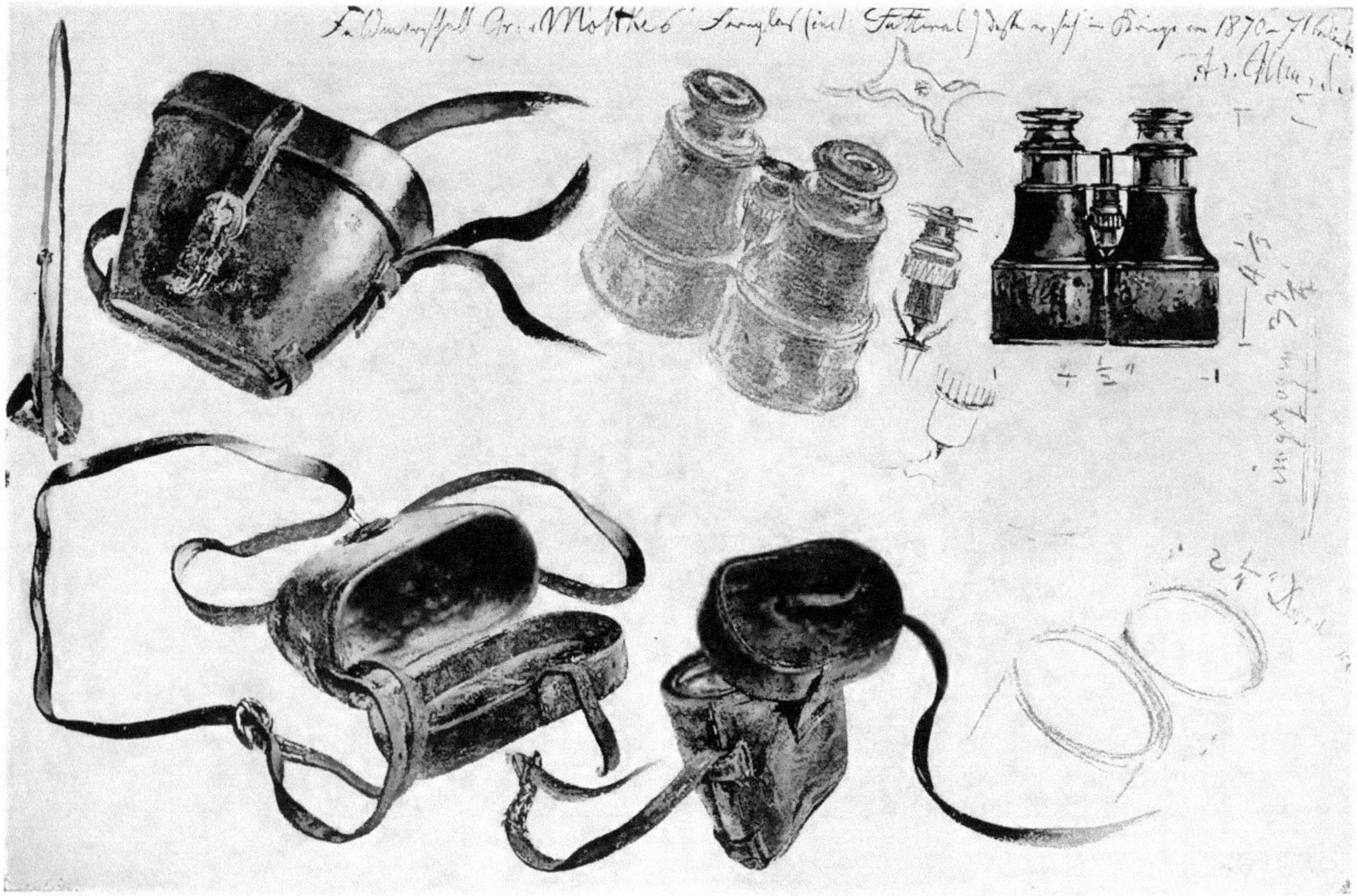

COUNT MOLTKE'S FIELD-GLASSES

PLATE XXII

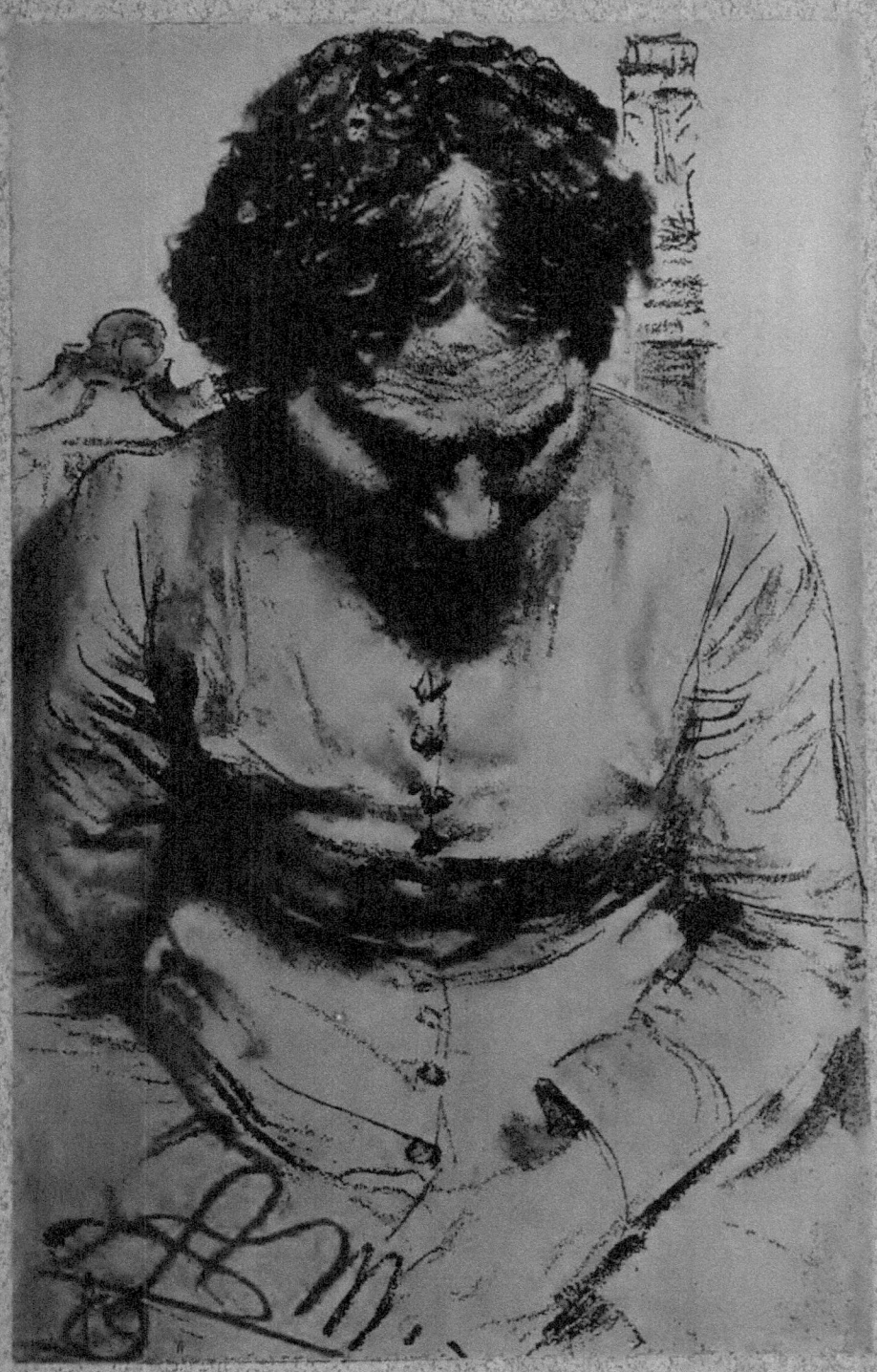

OLD LADY IN A HIGH-BACKED CHAIR

PLATE XXIII

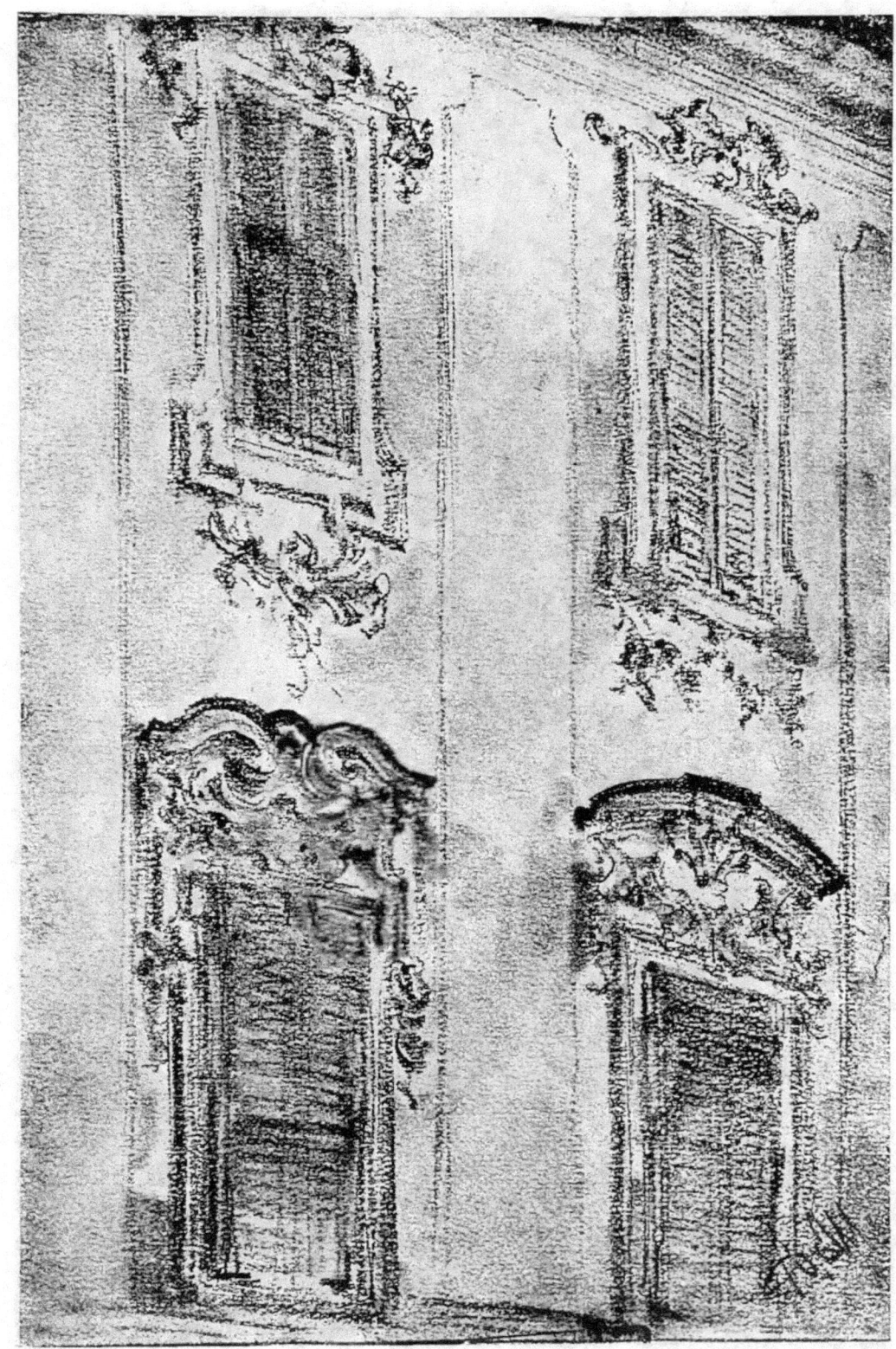

WINDOWS IN AN 18TH CENTURY HOUSE

PLATE XXIV

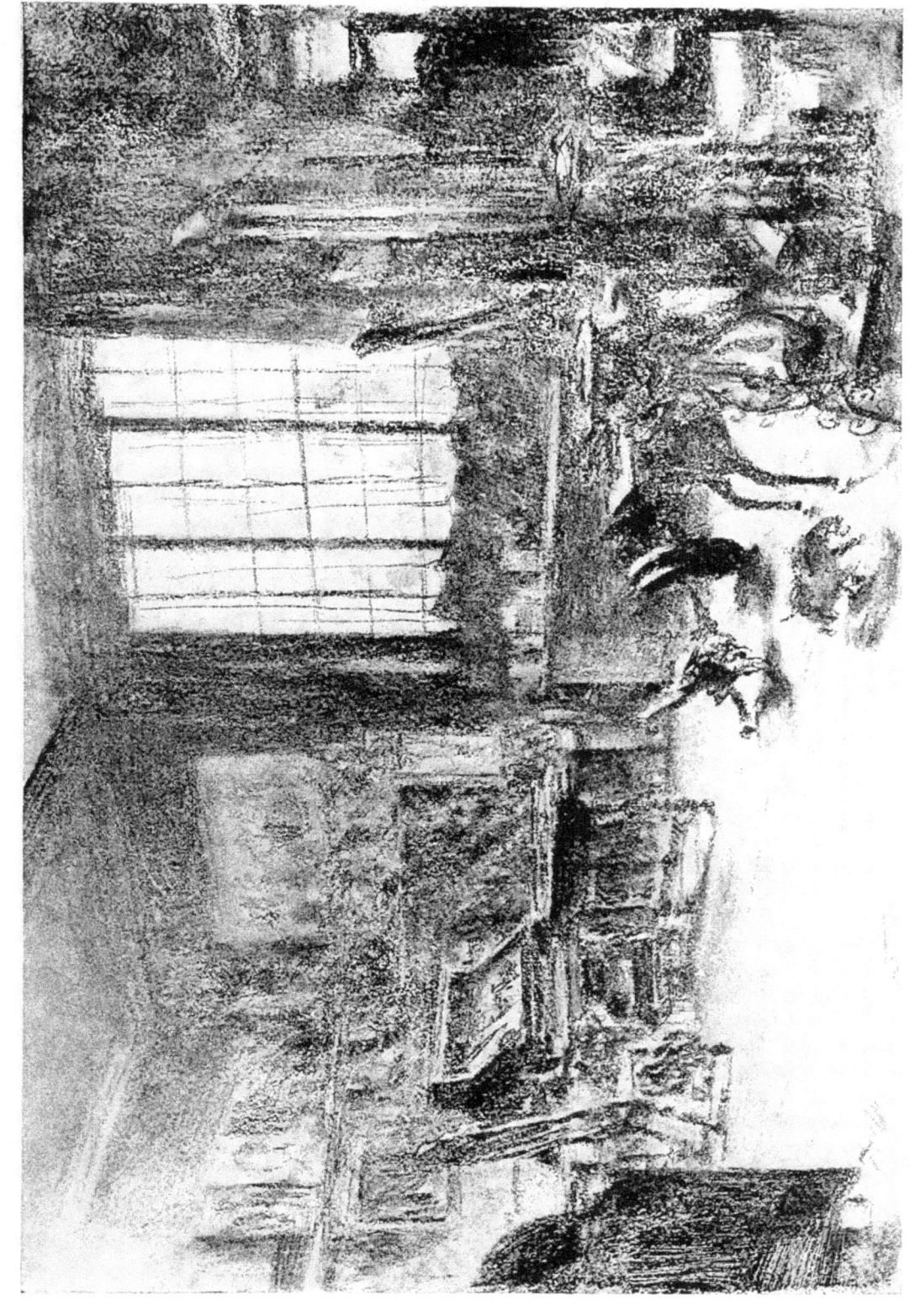

IMAGINARY SCENE IN MENZEL'S STUDIO, AFTER HIS DEATH

PLATE XXV

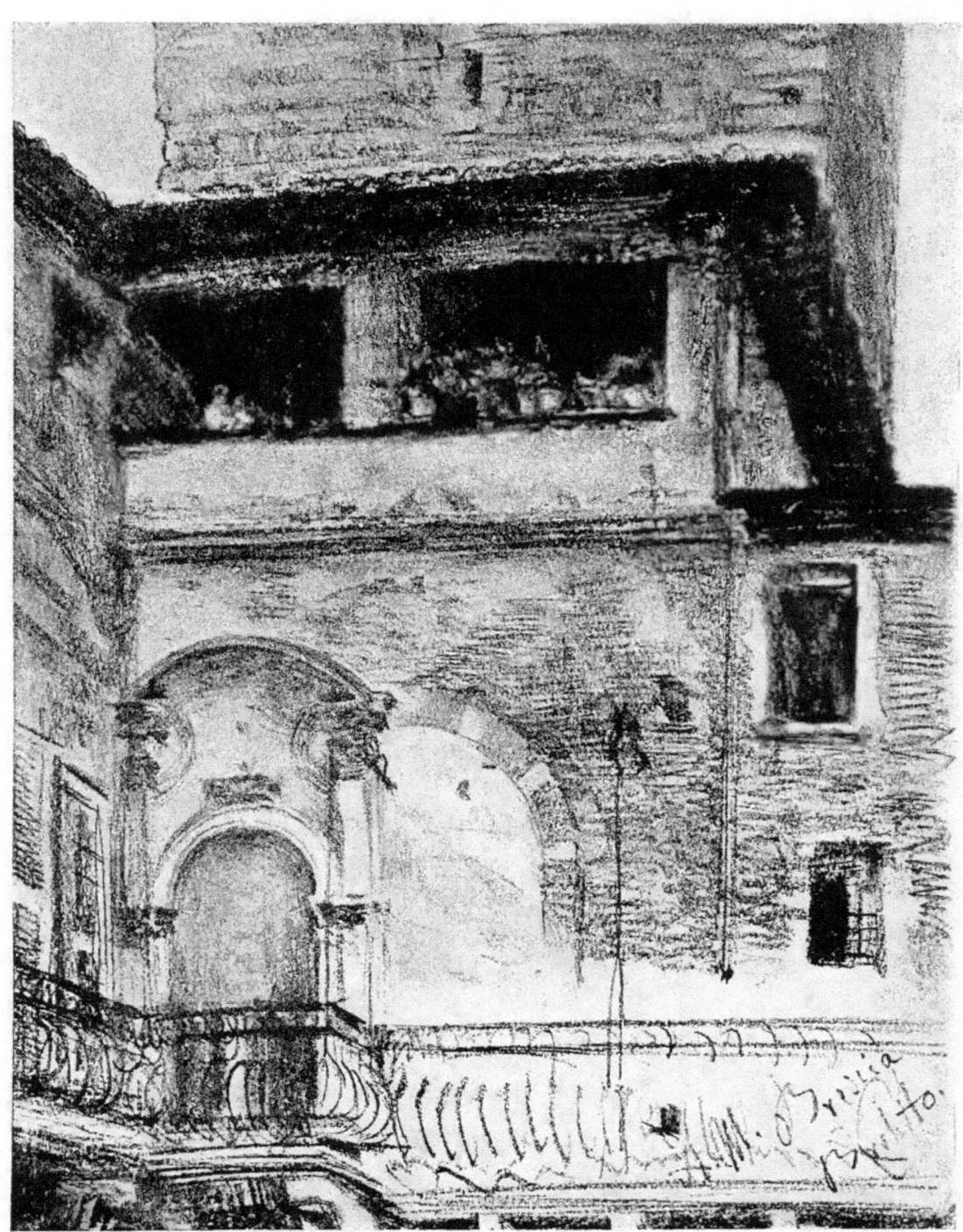

THE BROLETTO AT BRESCIA

PLATE XXVI

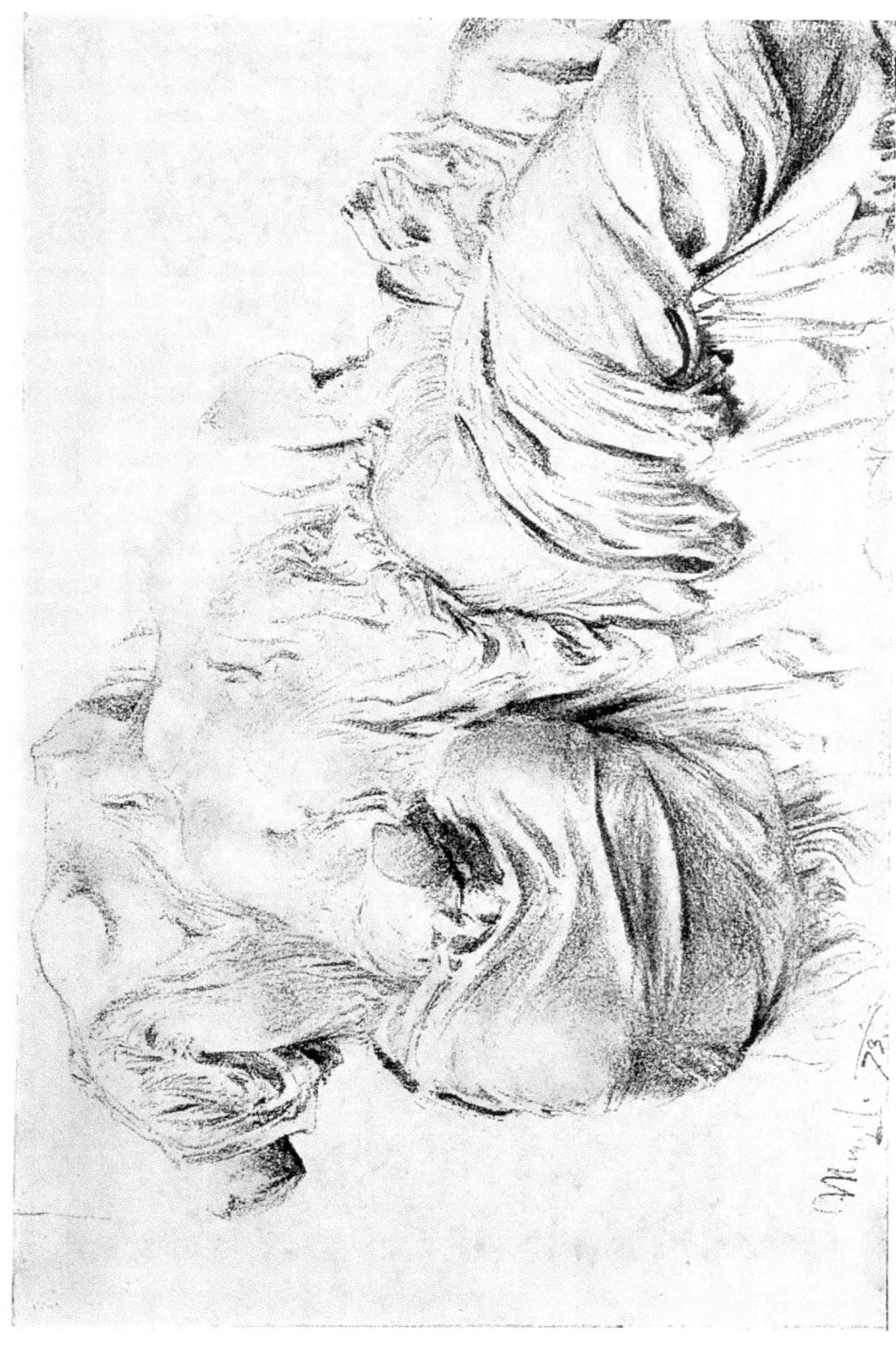

GROUP FROM THE PARTHENON SCULPTURES

PLATE XXVII

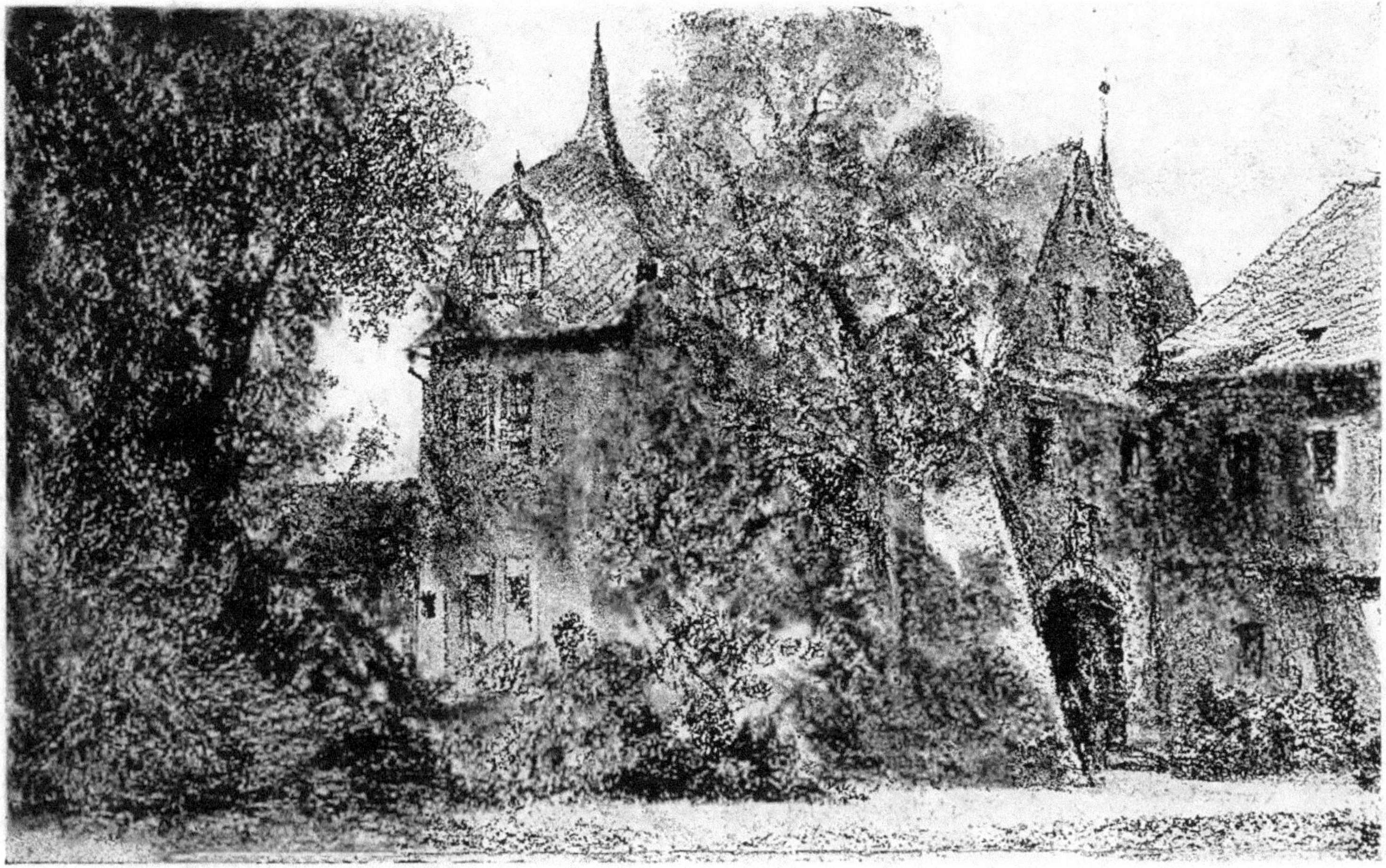

CHATEAU IN A PARK

PLATE XXVIII

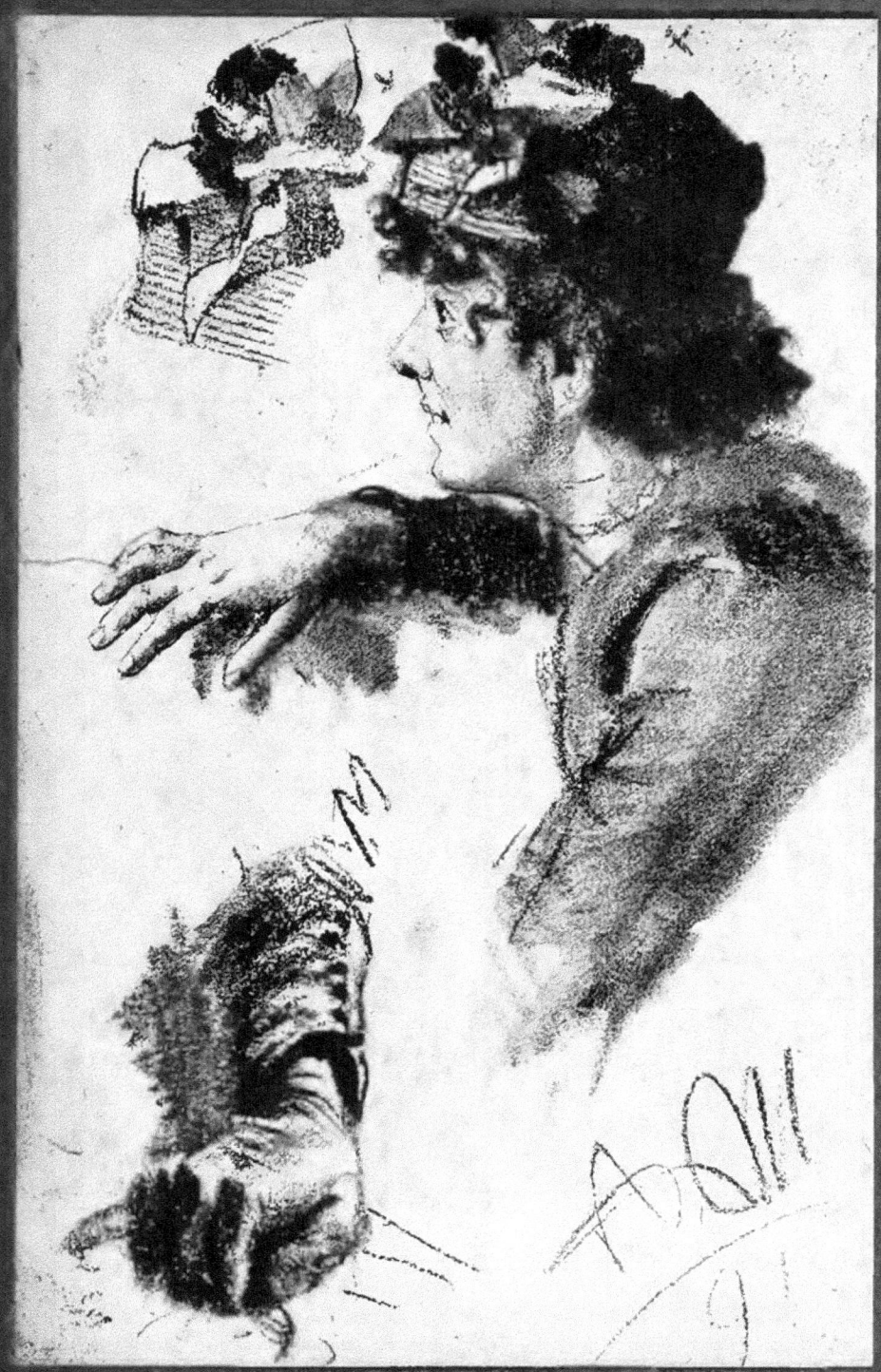

STUDIES OF A GIRL IN A HAT

PLATE XXIX

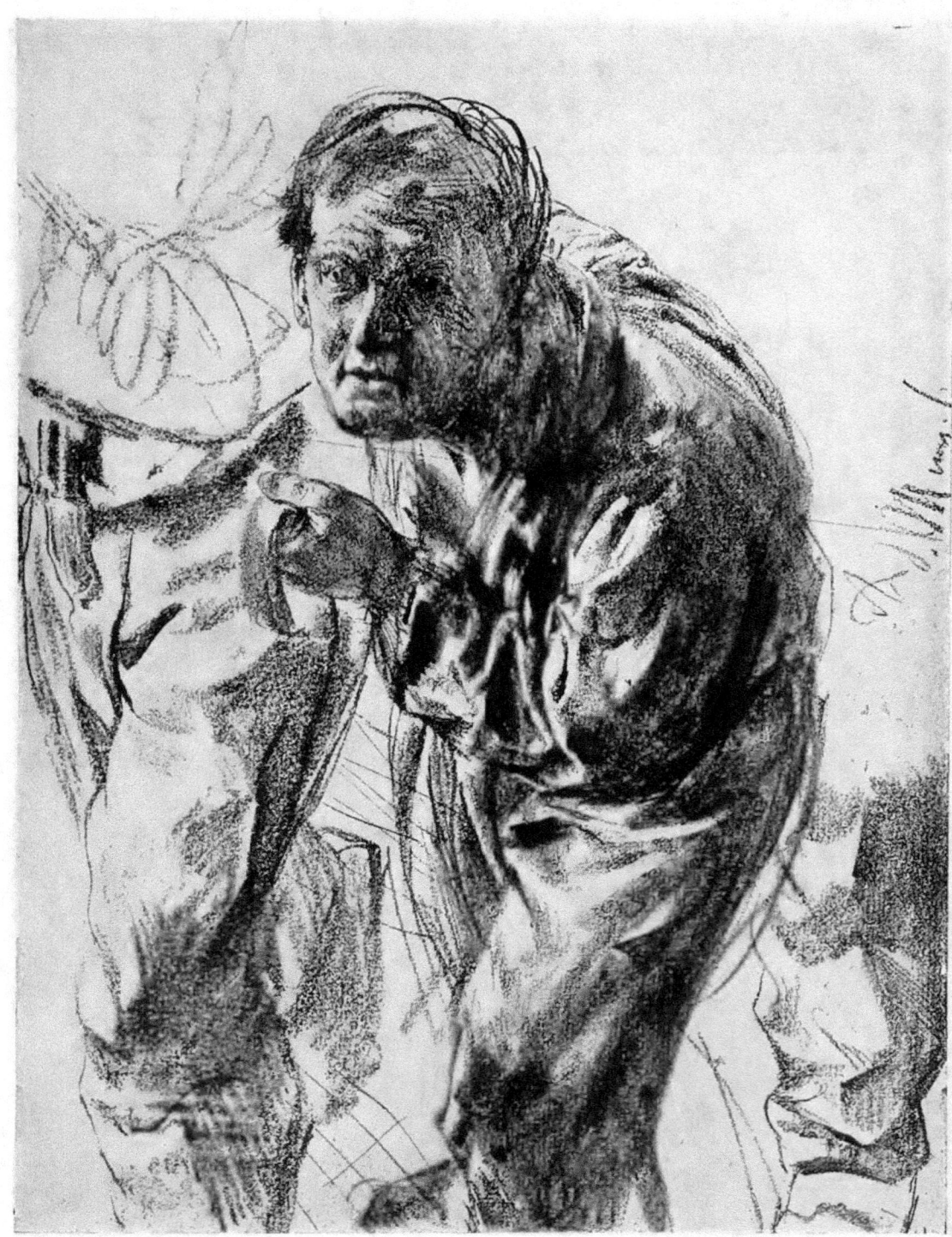

A MAN DRAWING A CART

PLATE XXX

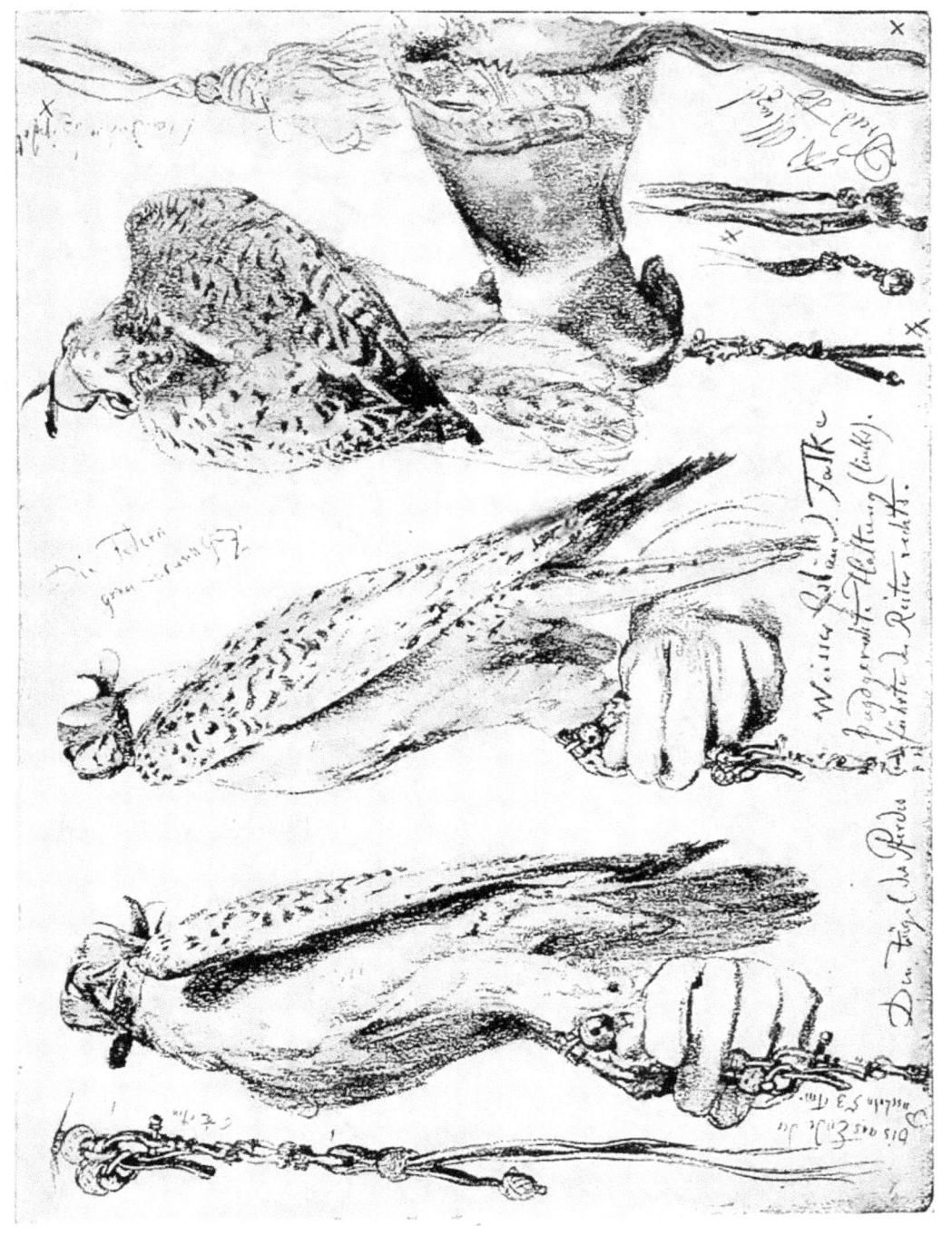

A HOODED FALCON

PLATE XXXI

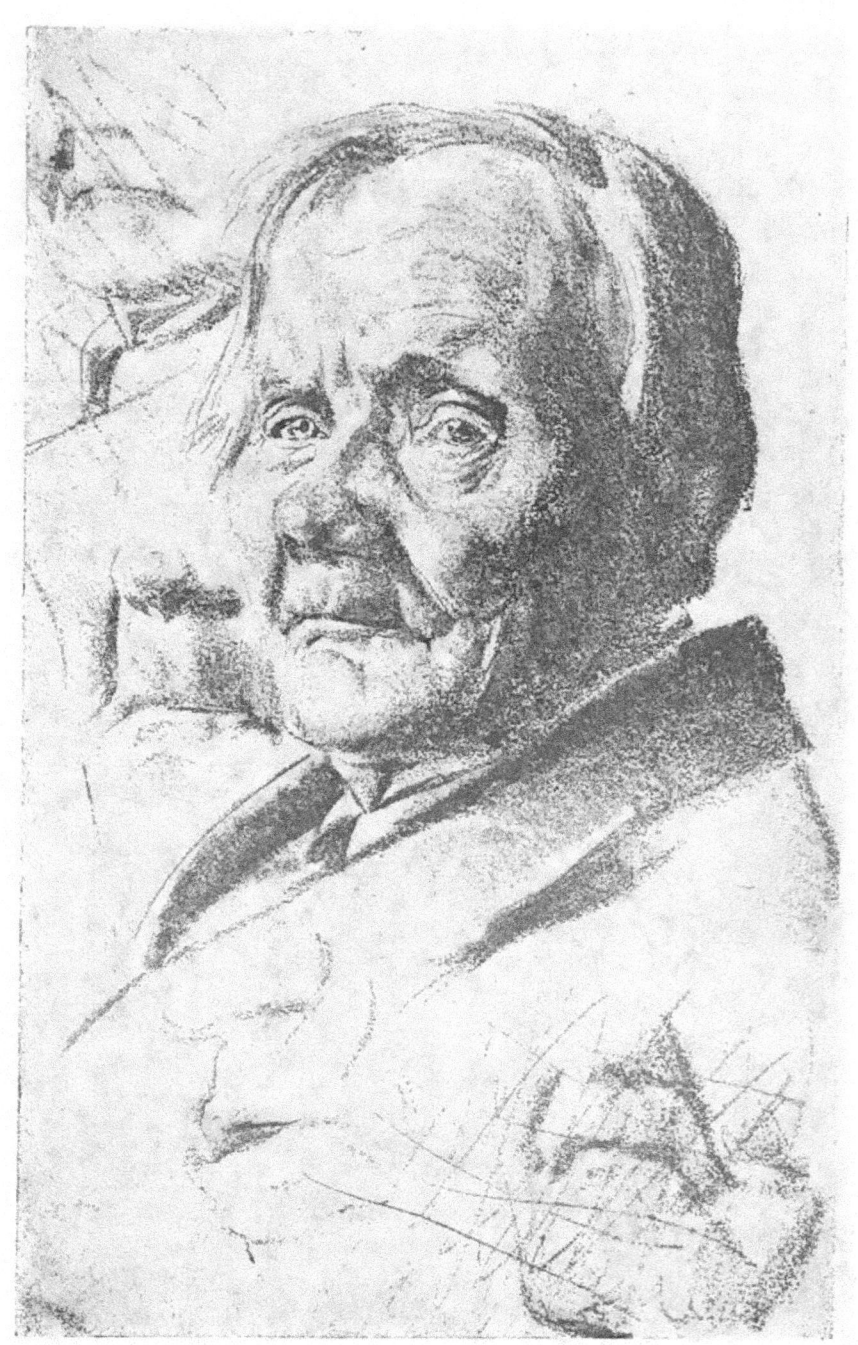

A MAN'S HEAD

PLATE XXXII

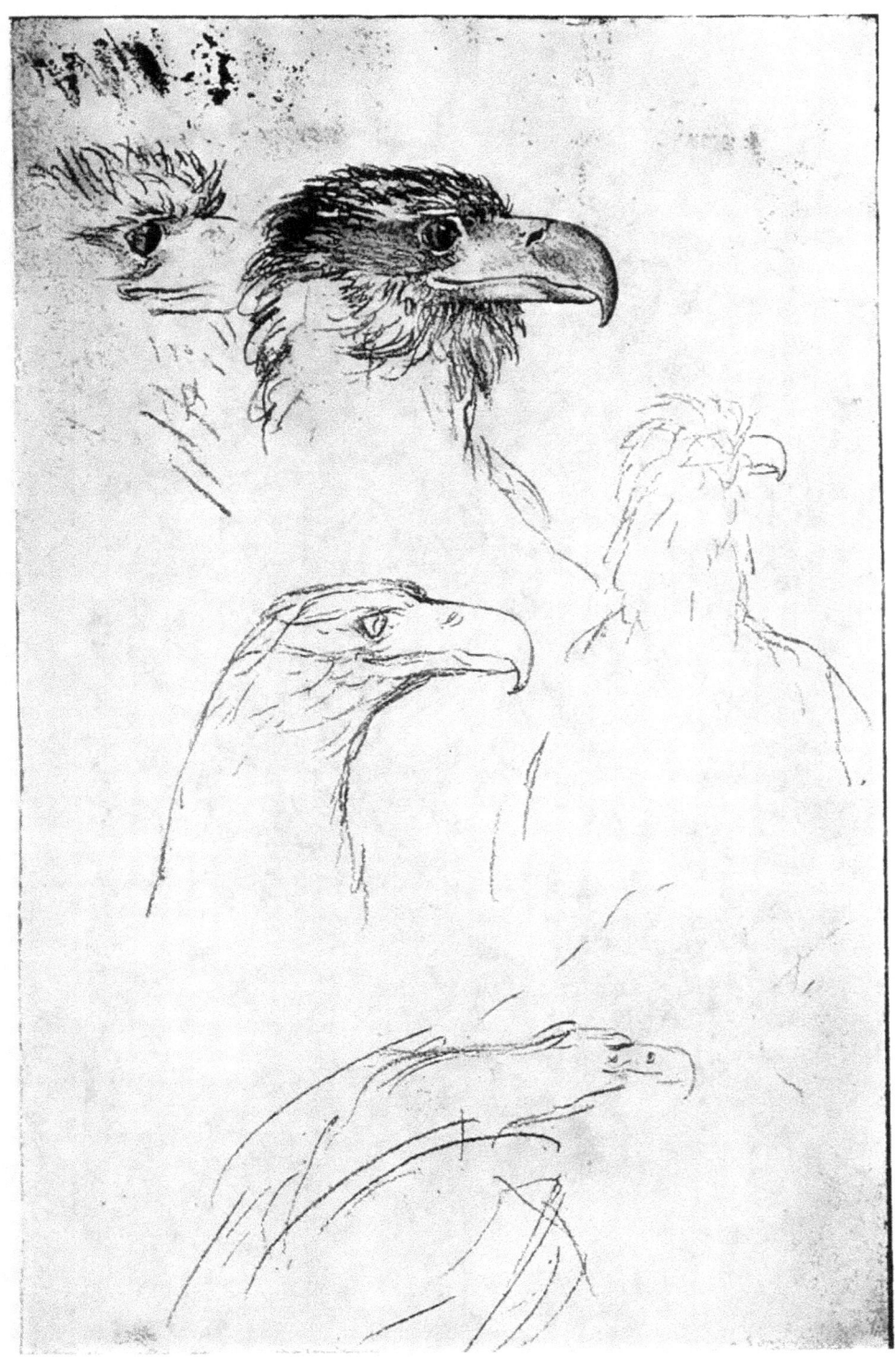

HEAD OF AN EAGLE

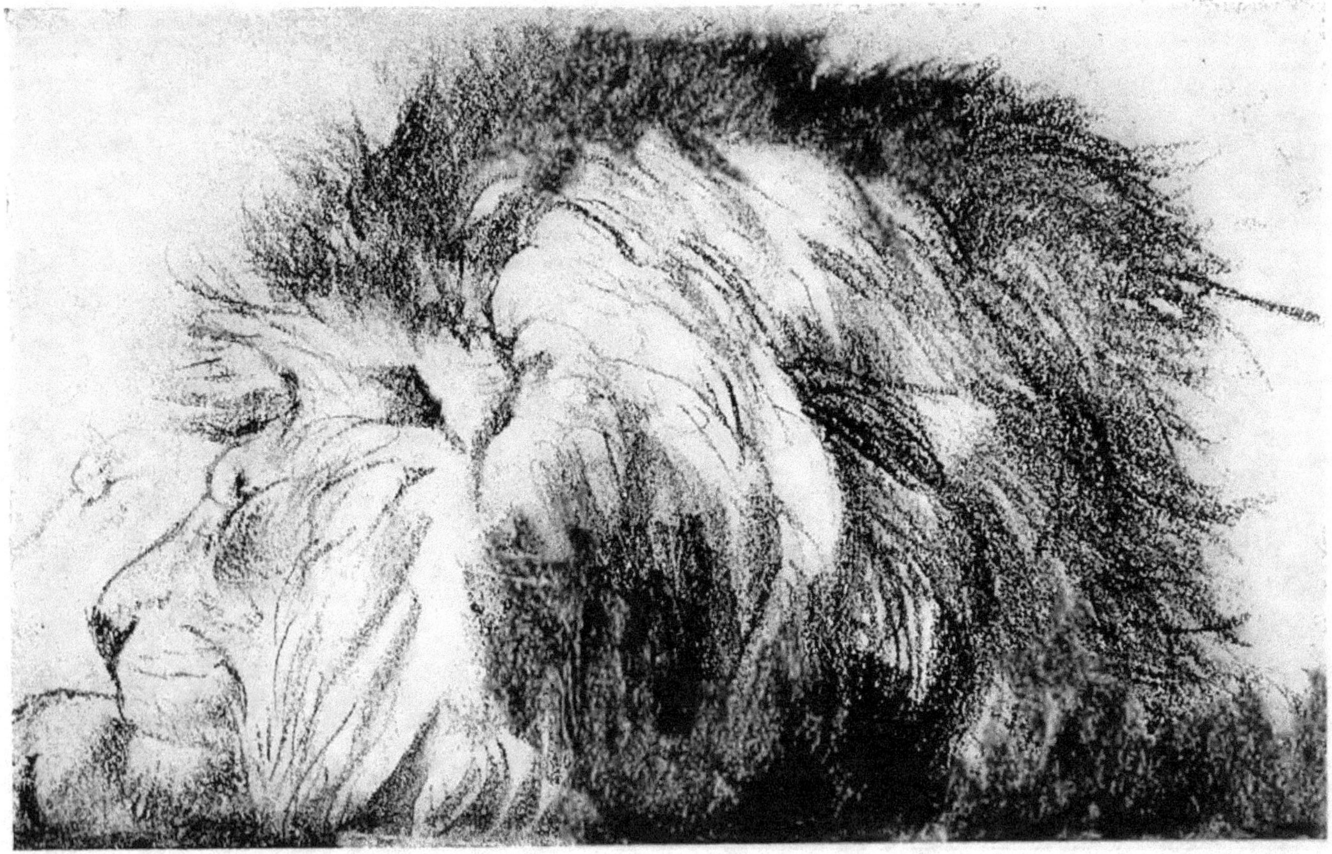

PLATE XXXIII

A SLEEPING LION'S HEAD

PLATE XXXIV

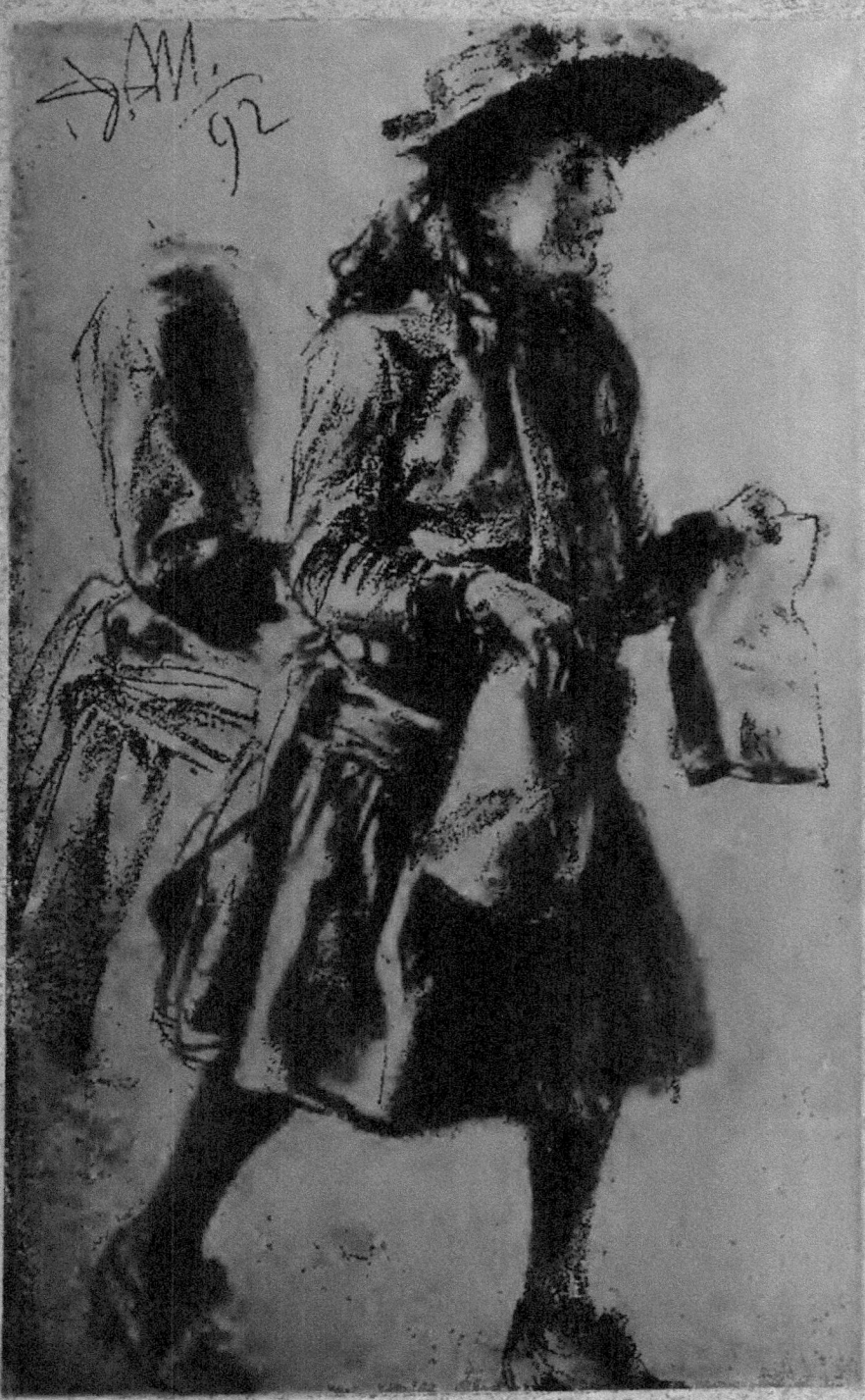

A GIRL WITH PAPER BAGS

PLATE XXXV

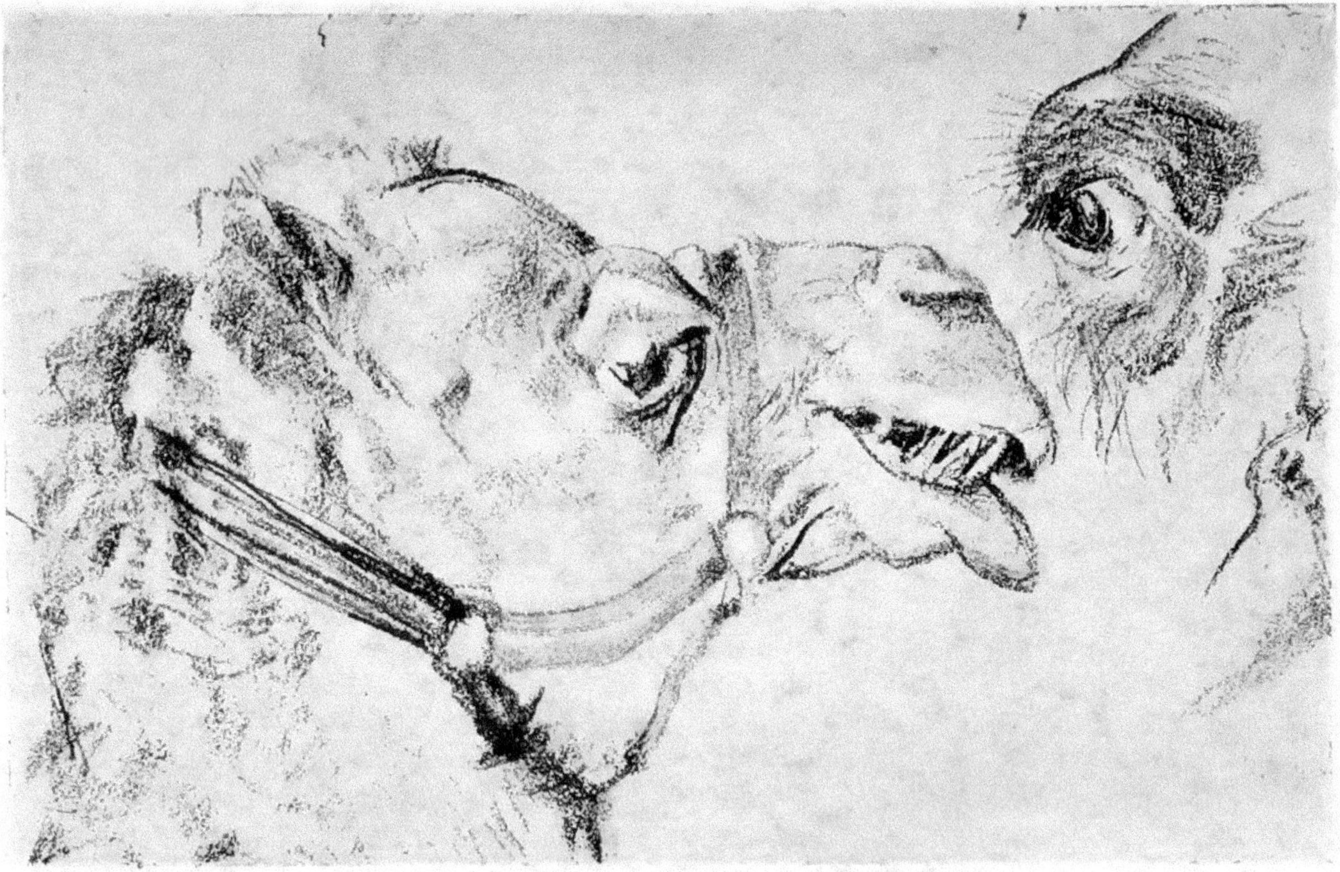

PLATE XXXVI

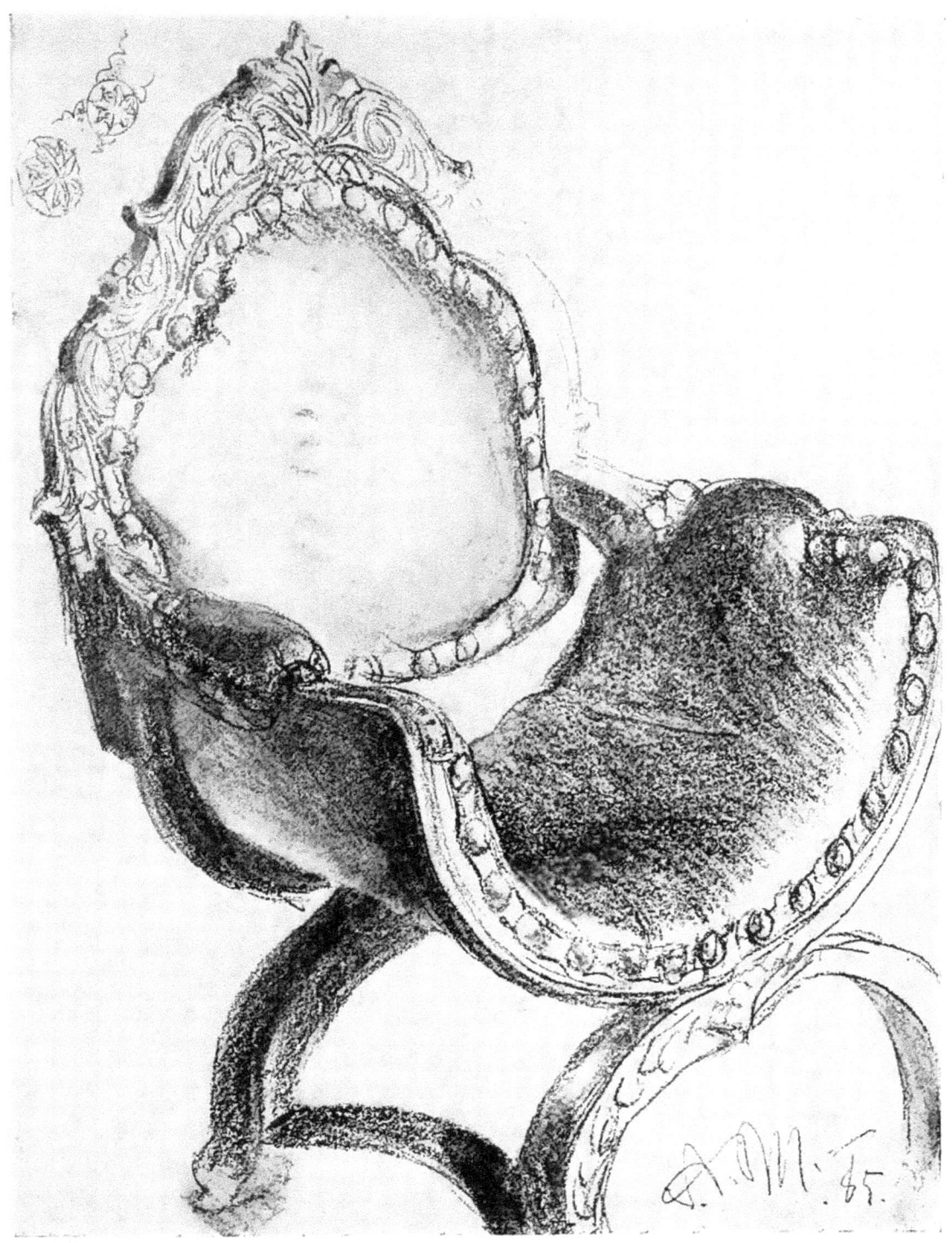

AN 18TH CENTURY ARM CHAIR

PLATE XXXVII

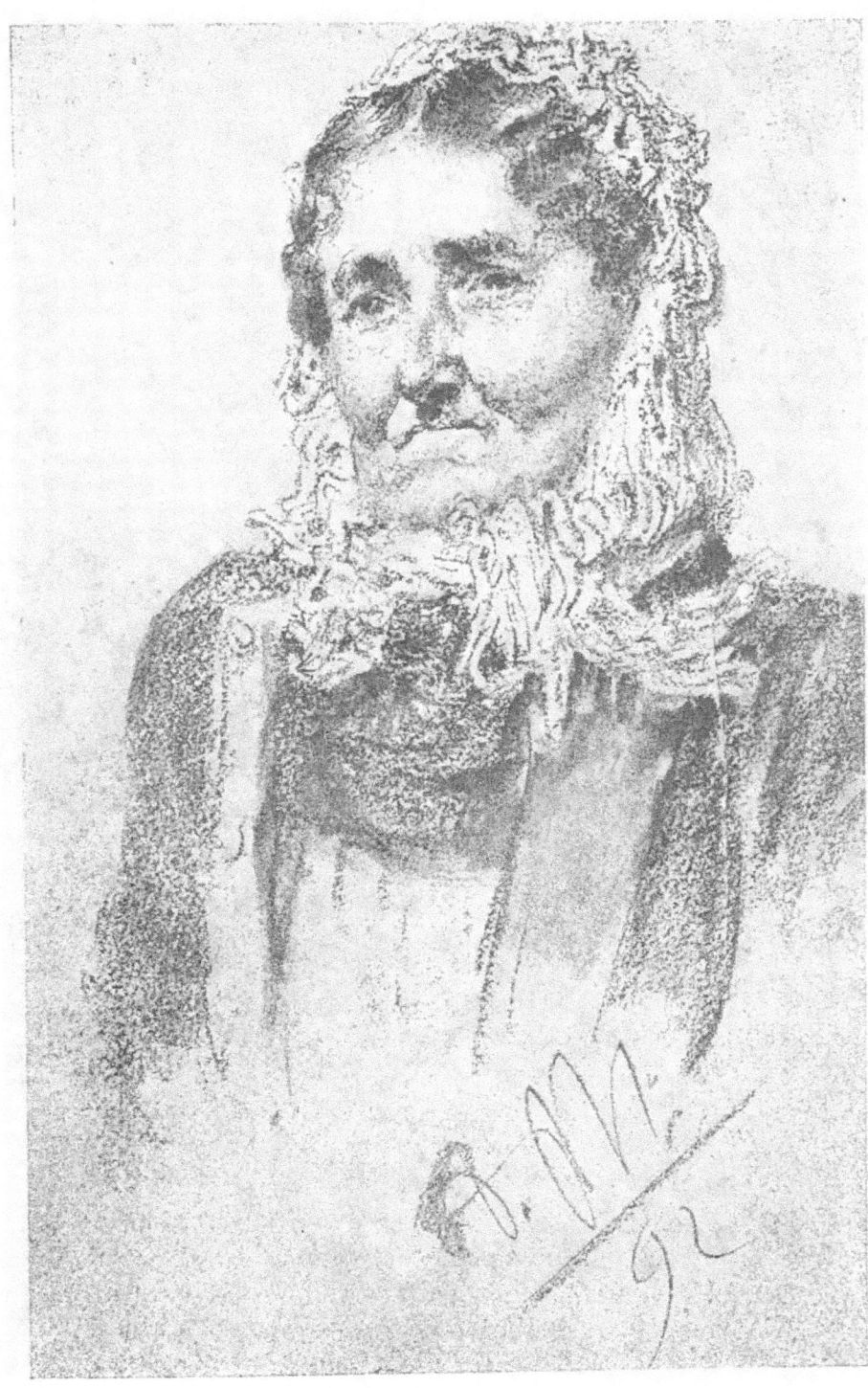

OLD LADY IN A CAP

PLATE XXXVIII

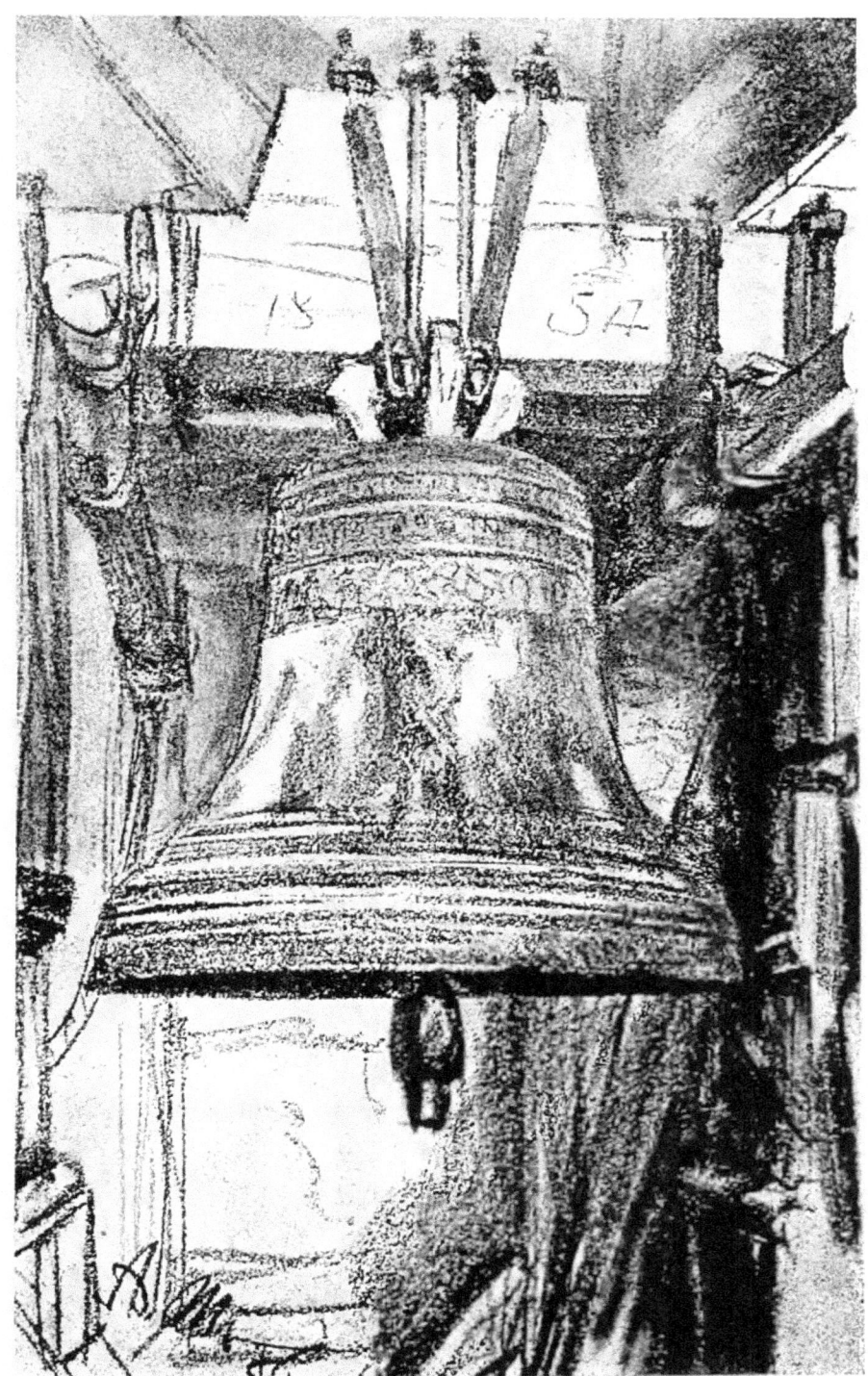

THE CHURCH BELL

PLATE XXXIX

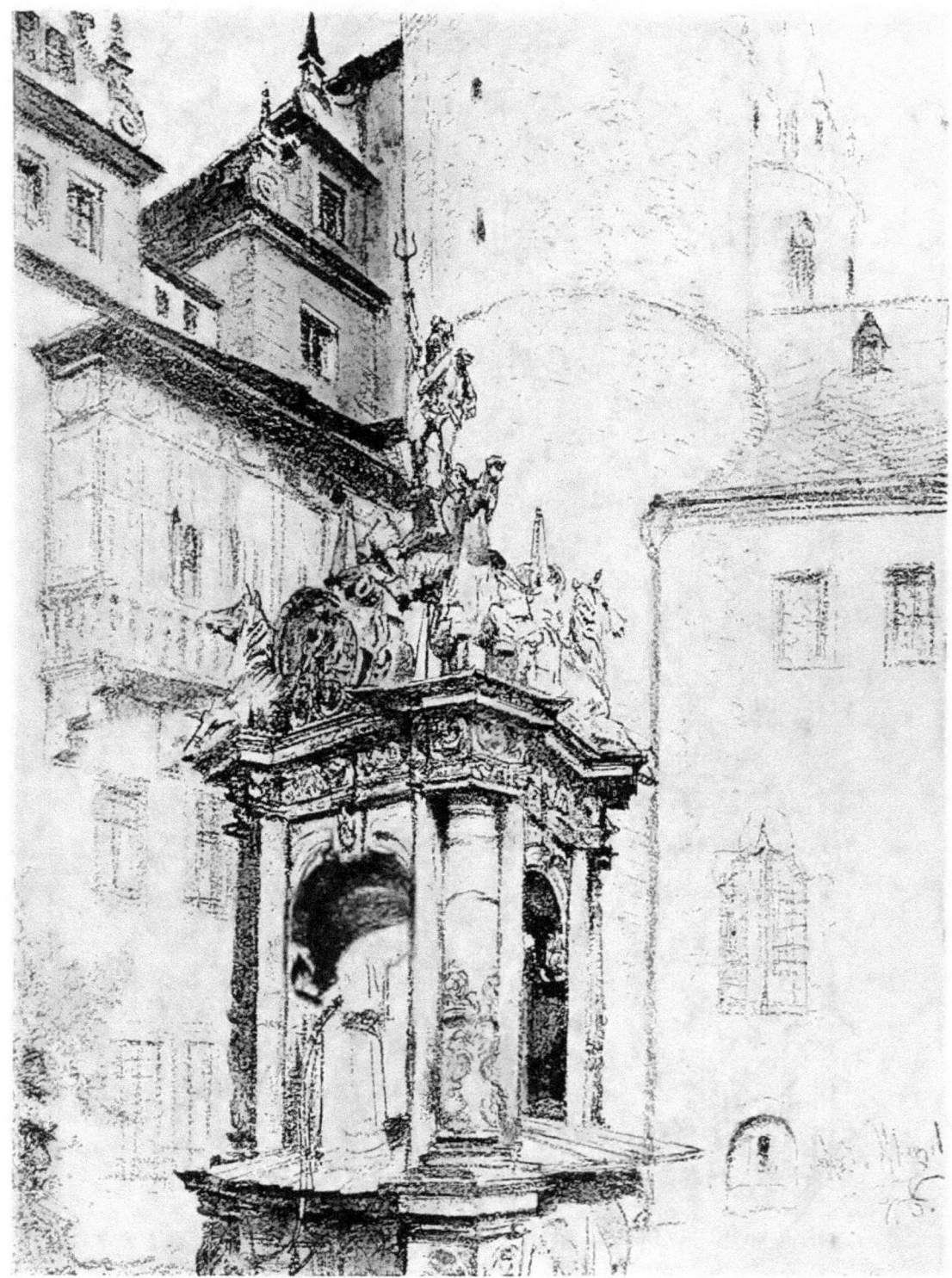

A NEPTUNE FOUNTAIN IN THE PALACE COURTYARD AT MERSEBURG

PLATE XL

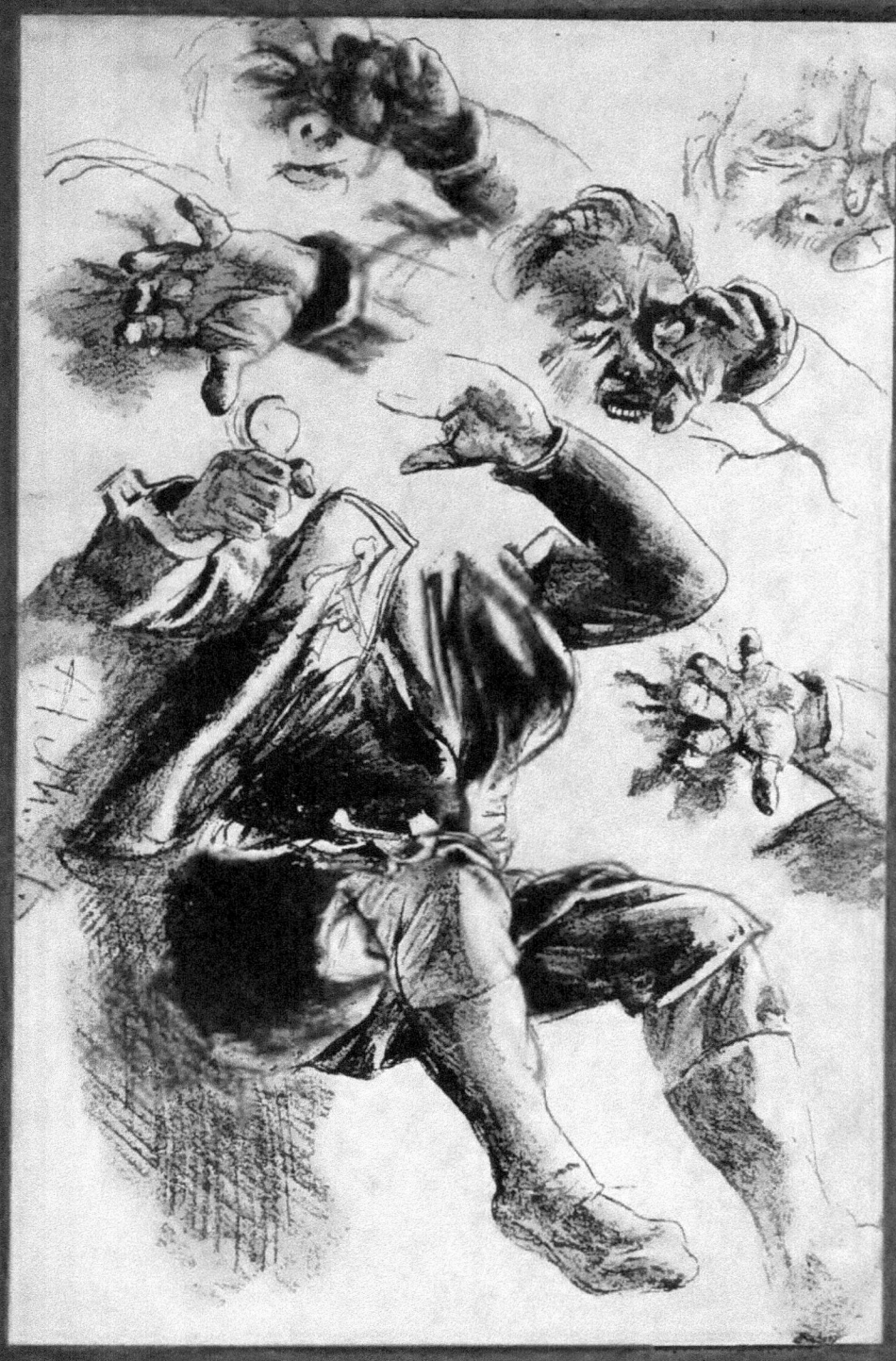

STUDIES FOR A BOY CRYING

PLATE XLI

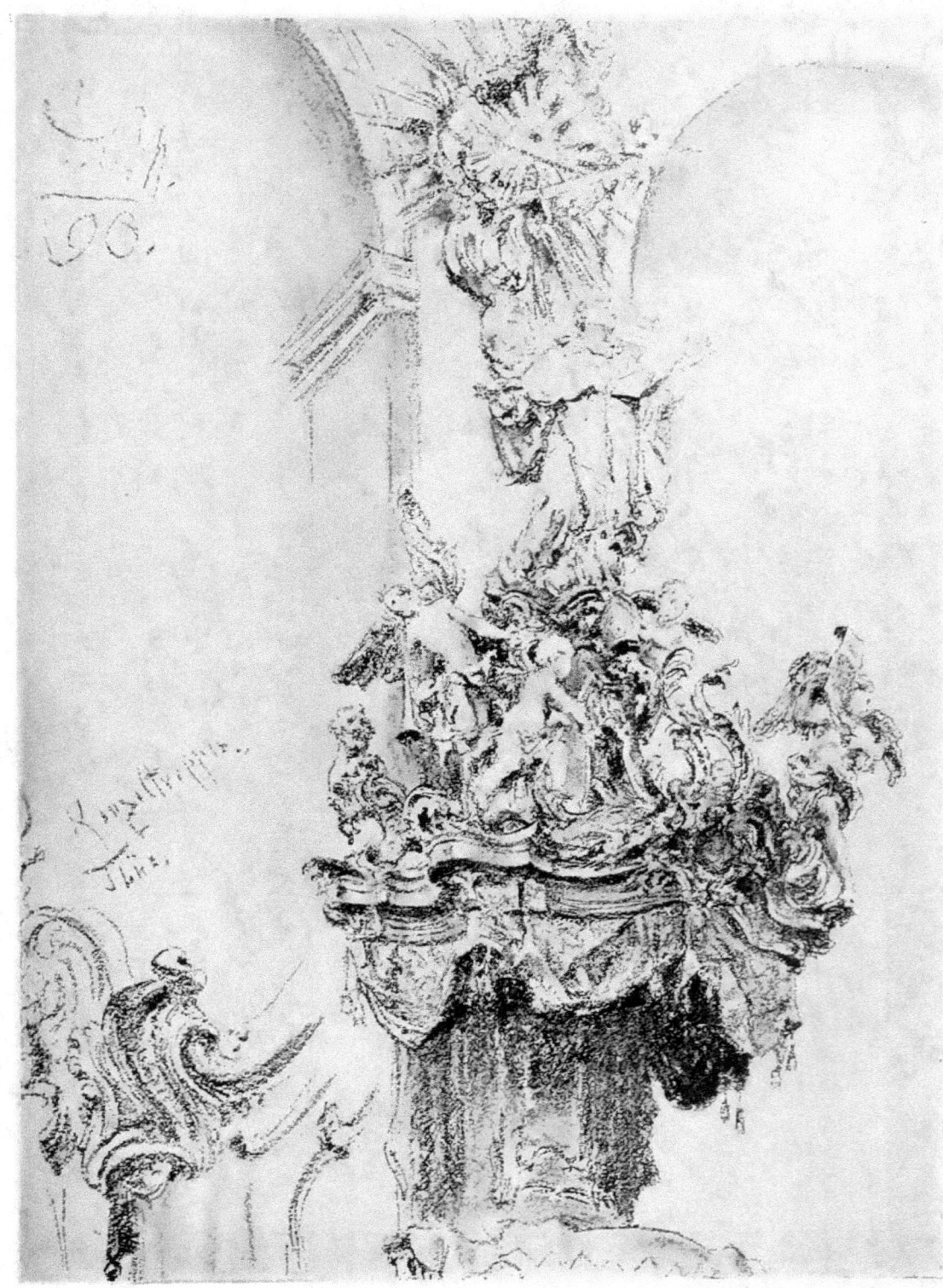

TOP OF THE PULPIT IN THE CATHEDRAL AT WÜRZBURG

PLATE XLII

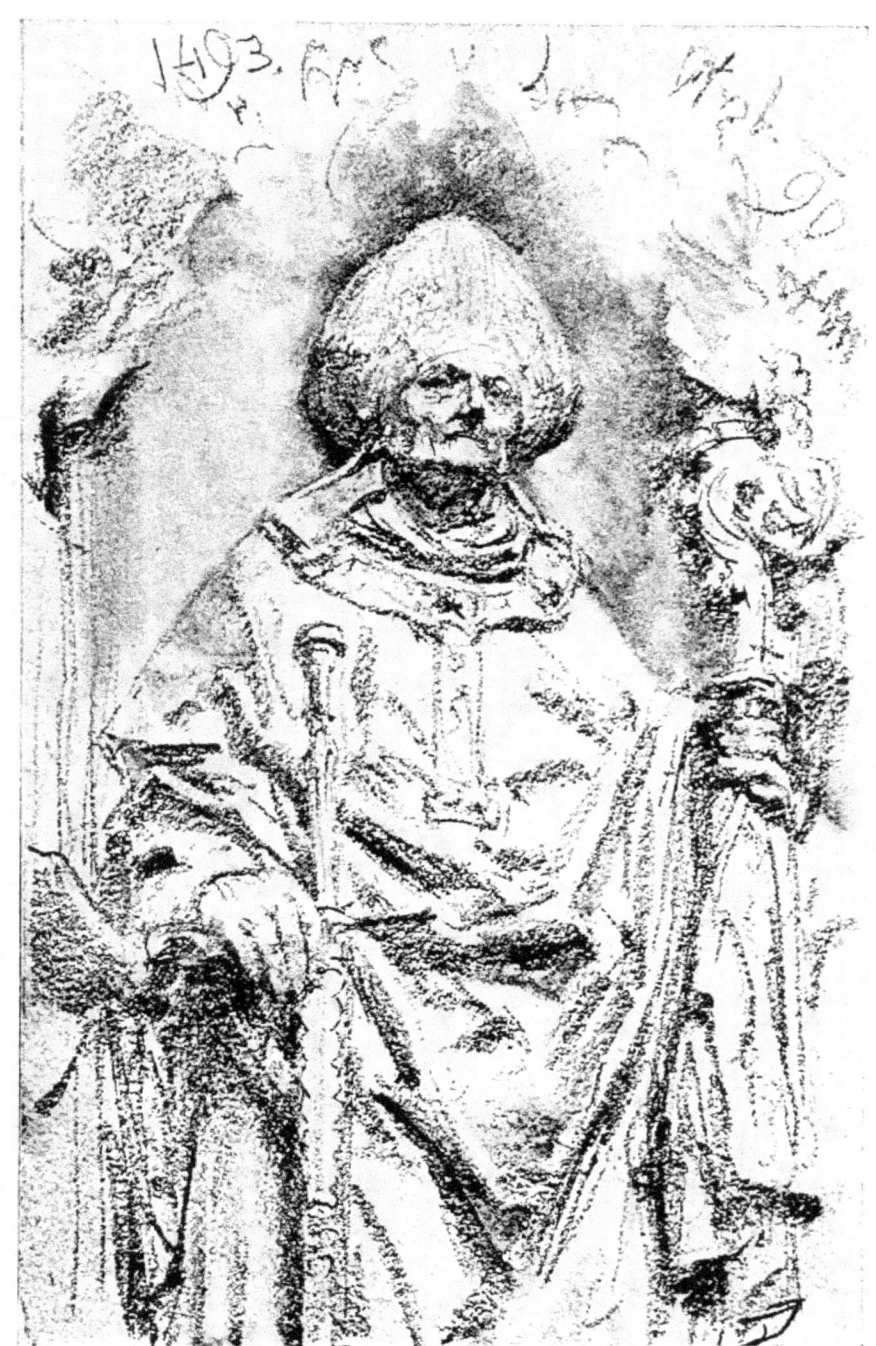

TOMBSTONE OF A BISHOP IN THE
CATHEDRAL AT WÜRZBURG

PLATE XLIII

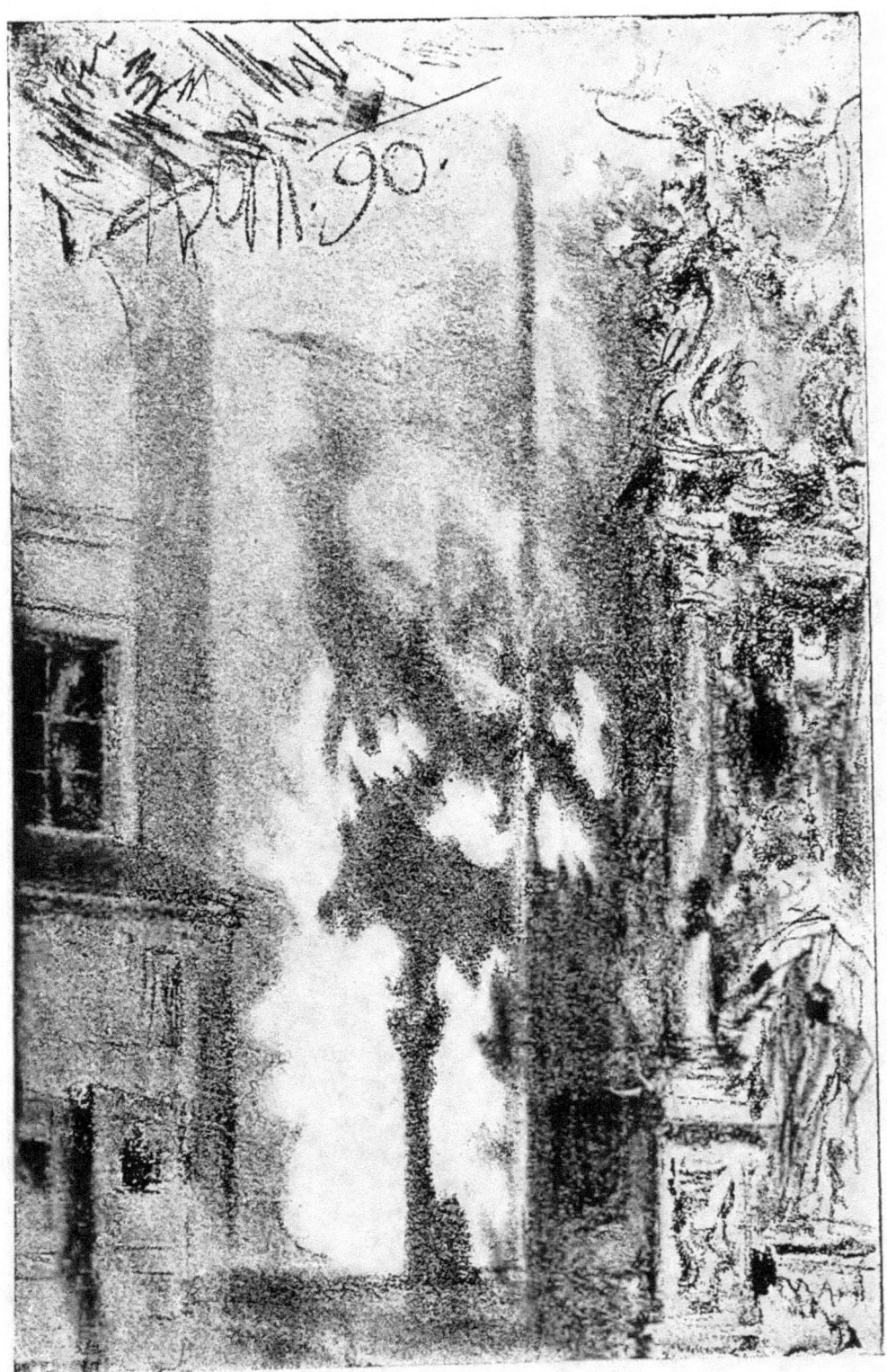

INTERIOR OF A CHURCH AT WÜRZBURG

PLATE XLIV

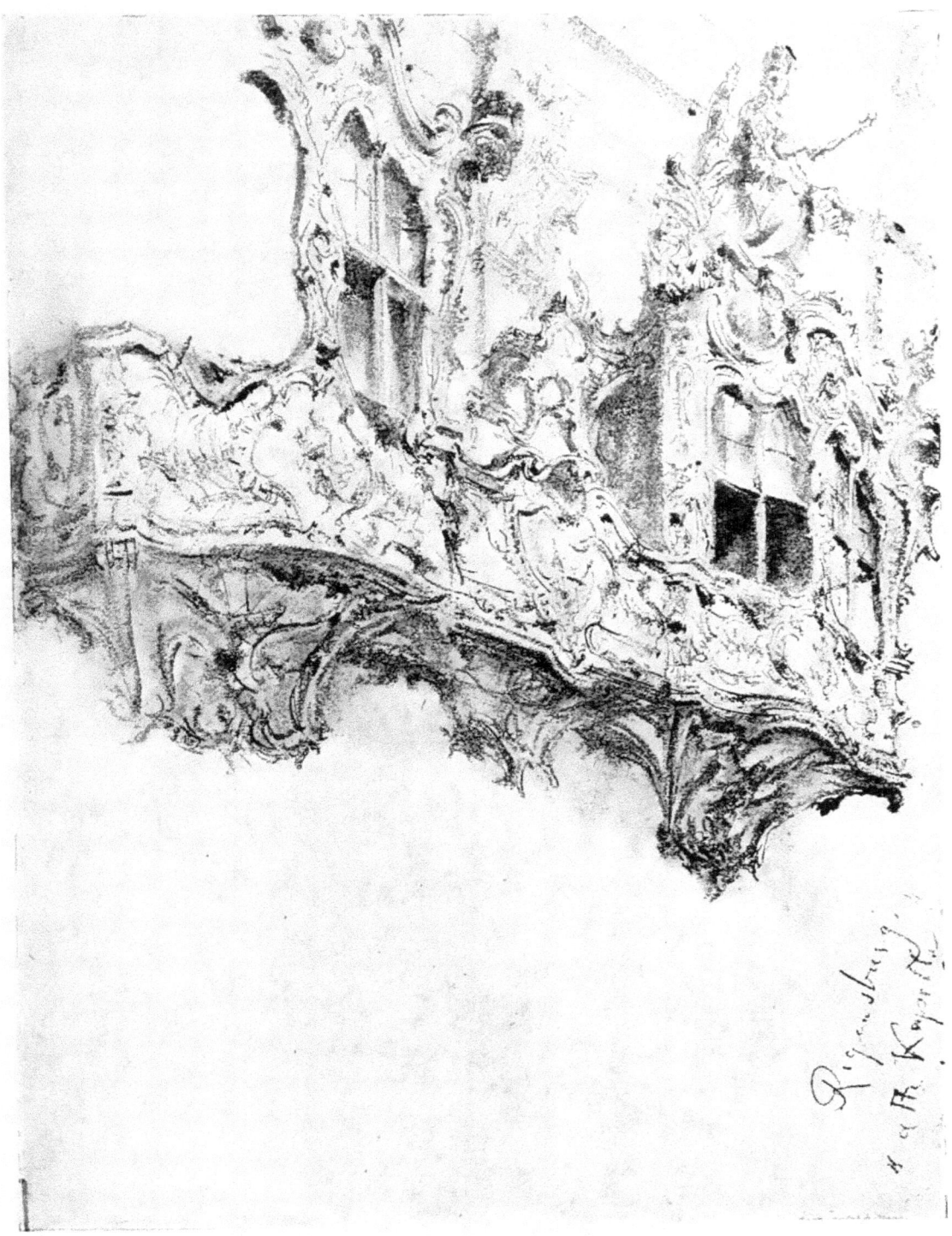

LOFT IN THE ALL SAINTS' CHAPEL AT RATISBON

PLATE XLV

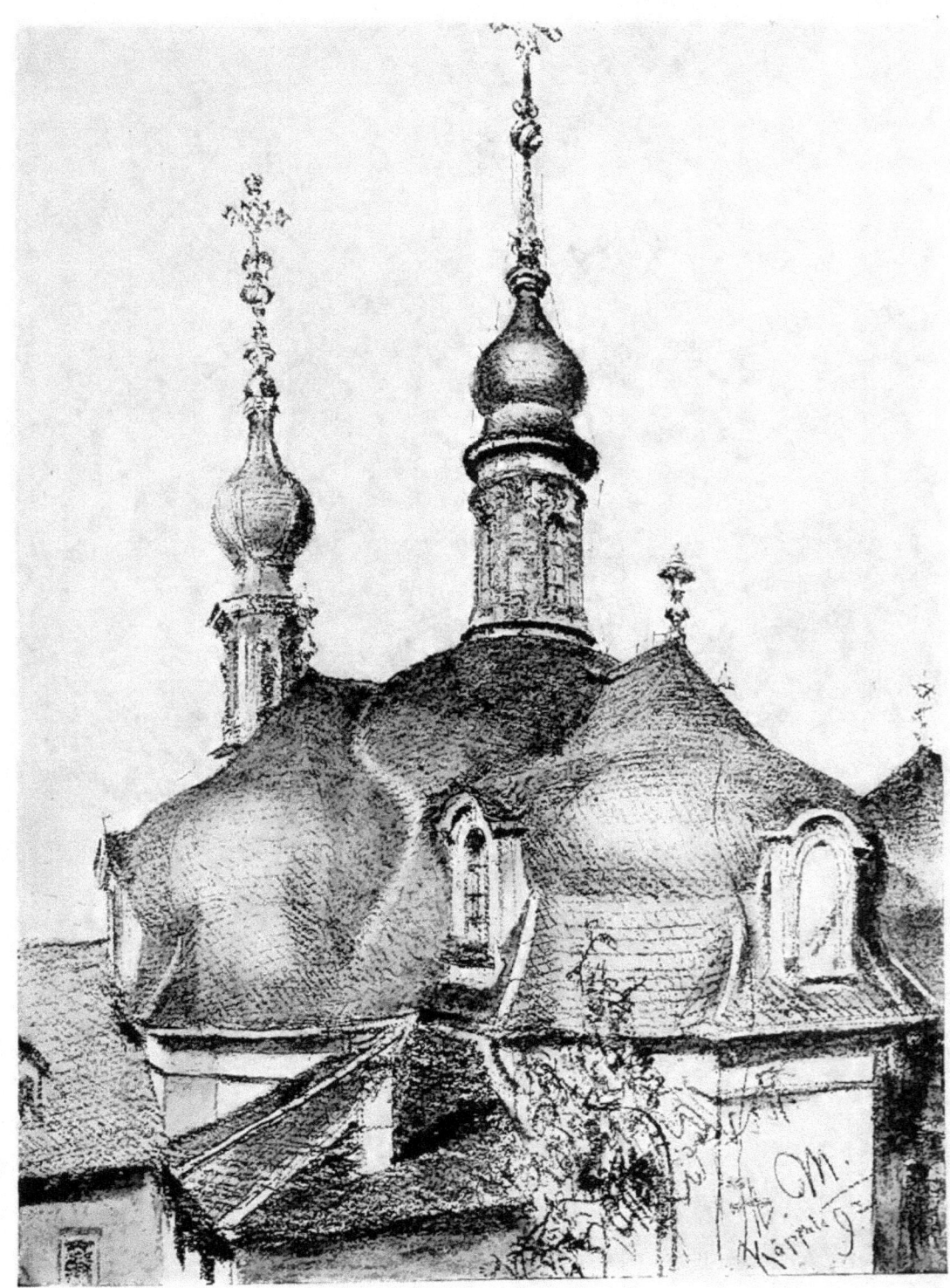

THE TURRETS OF THE CHAPEL AT WÜRZBURG

PLATE XLVI

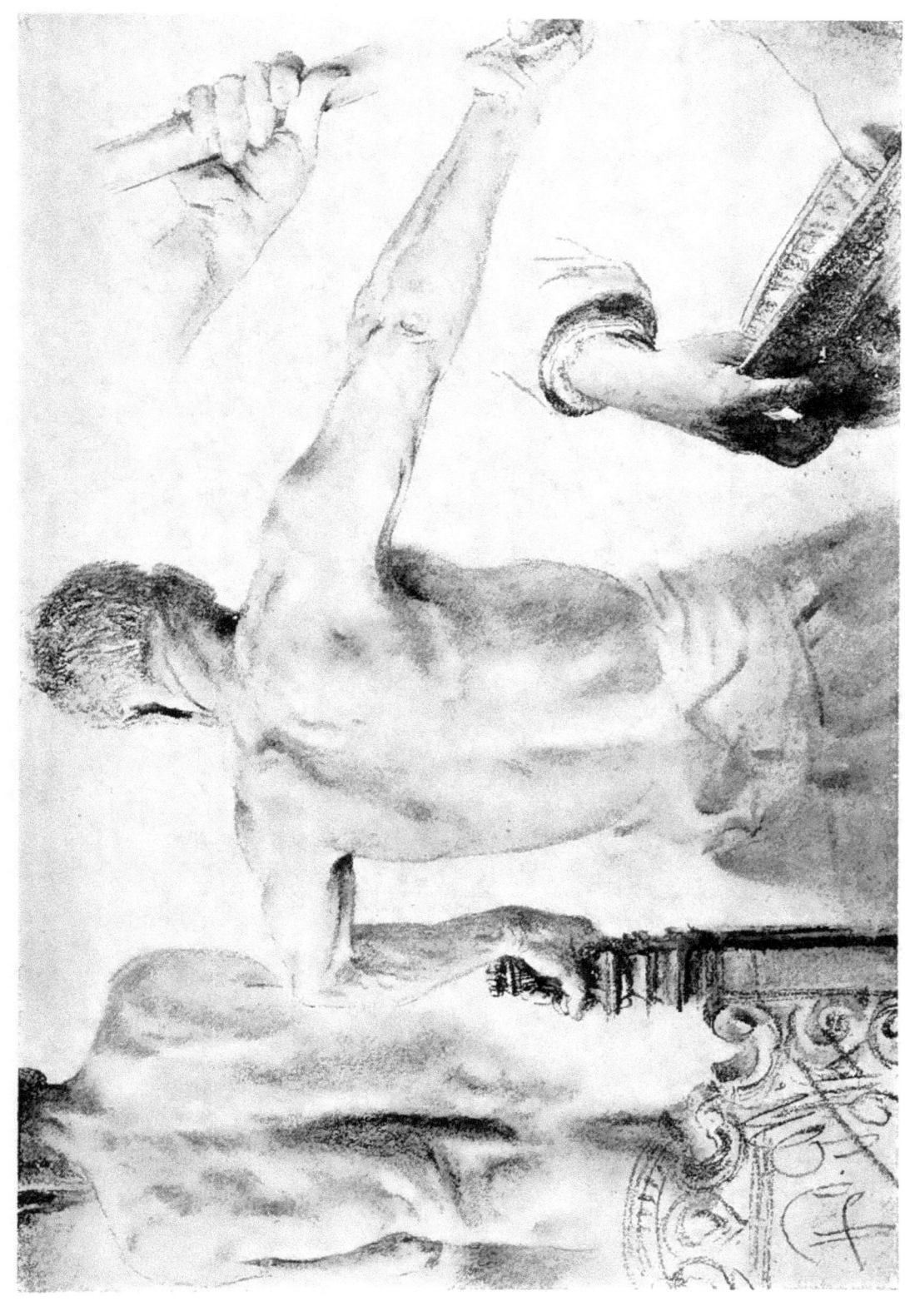

STUDIES OF A MAN'S BACK, A WOMAN'S HAND, ETC.

PLATE XLVII

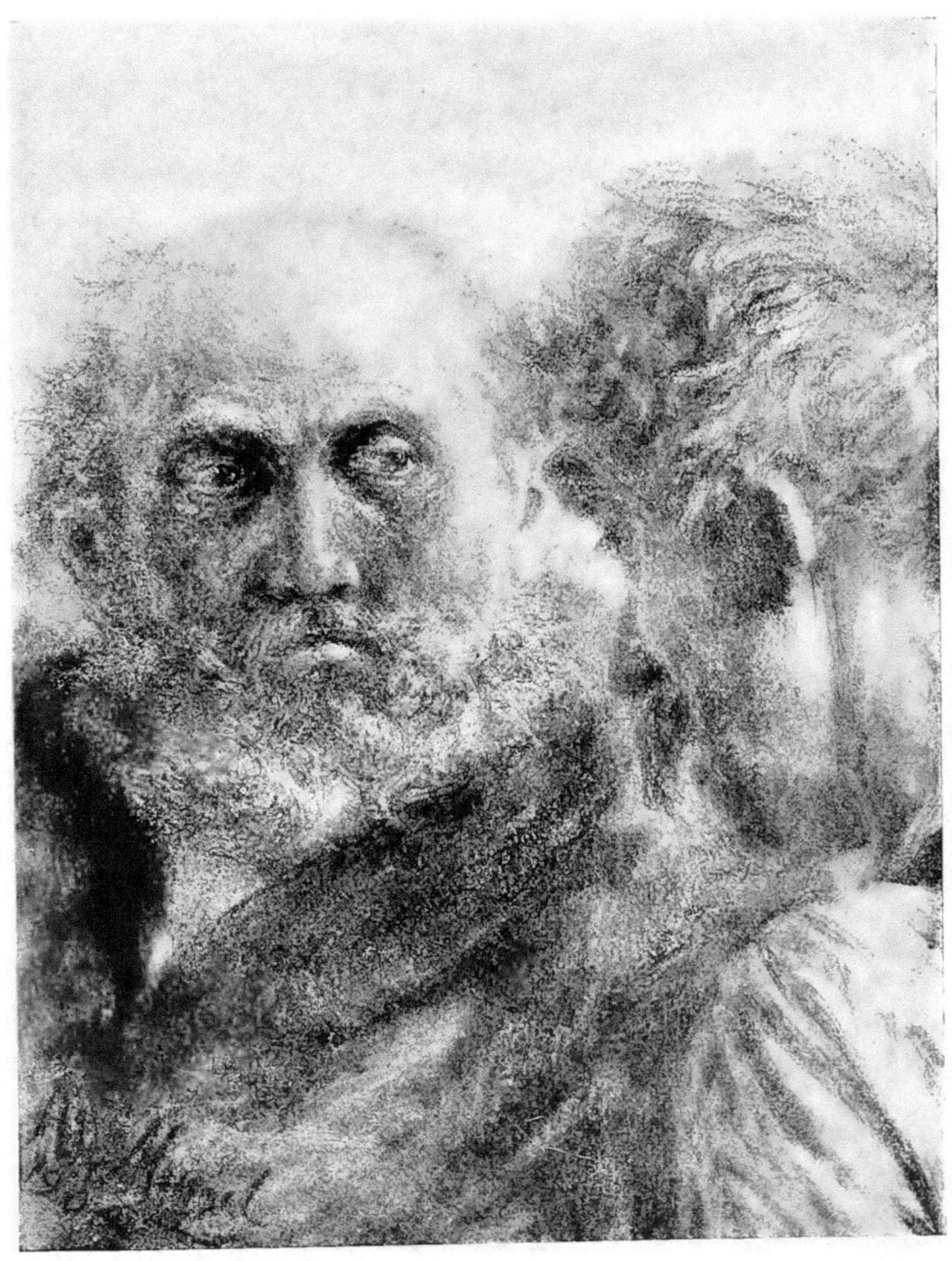

STUDIES OF TWO HEADS

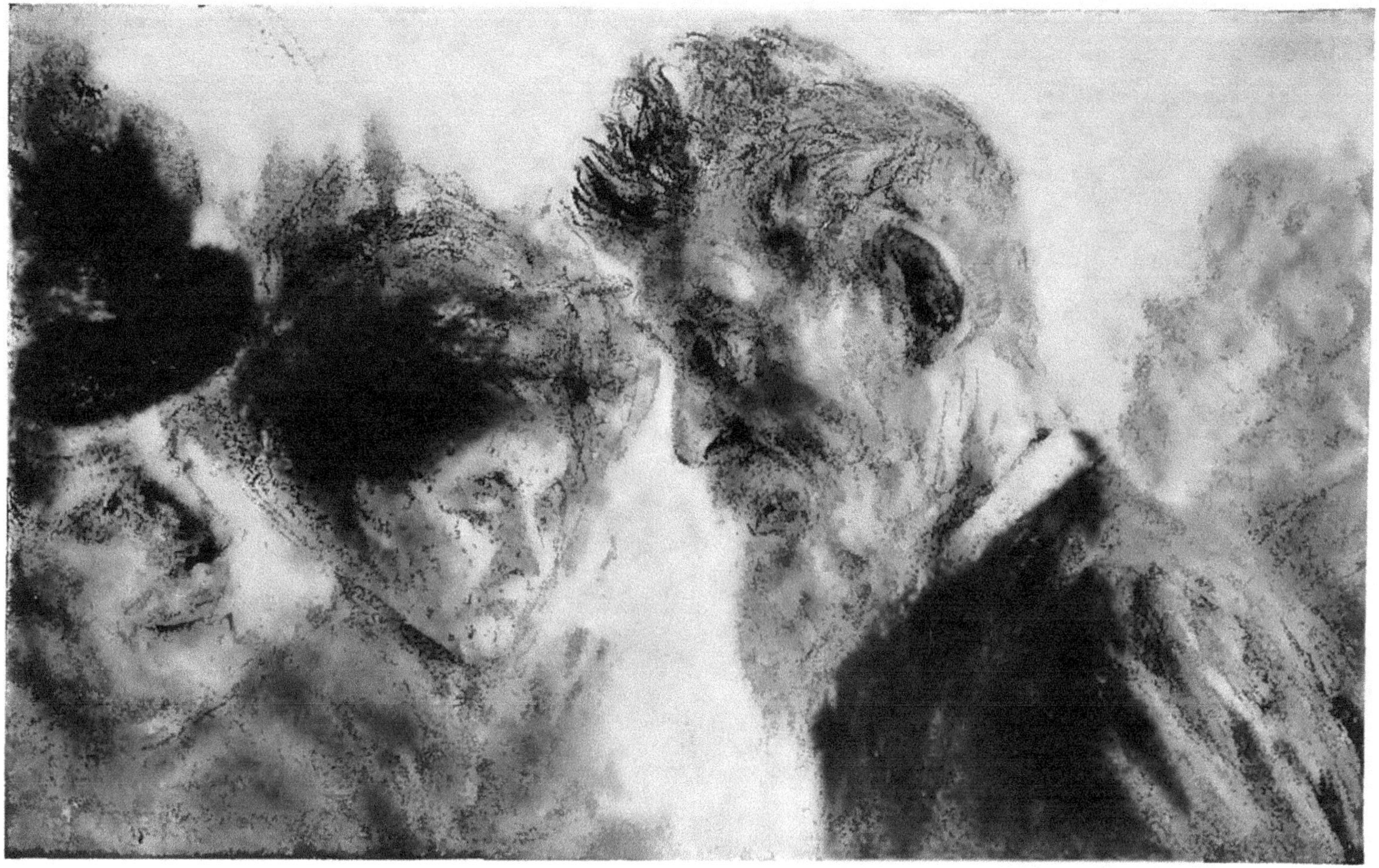

PLATE XLVIII

TWO LADIES AND A GENTLEMAN